*Fair to Middlin'*

# Fair to Middlin'

The Antebellum Cotton Trade
of the
Apalachicola/Chattahooche
River Valley

*Lynn Willoughby*

The University of Alabama Press
Tuscaloosa

*Recipient of the Mrs. Simon Baruch University Award*
*of the United Daughters of the Confederacy*

Copyright © 1993
The University of Alabama Press
Tuscaloosa, Alabama 35487-0380
All rights reserved
Manufactured in the United States of America

*designed by Paula C. Dennis*

∞

The paper on which this book is printed meets the minimum requirements of
American National Standard for Information Science-Permanence of Paper for
Printed Library Materials, ANSI Z39.48-1984

Library of Congress Cataloging-in-Publication Data

Willoughby, Lynn, 1951–
    Fair to middlin' : the antebellum cotton trade of the
Apalachicola/Chattahoochee River Valley  /  Lynn Willoughby.
        p. cm.
    Incudes bibliographical references and index.
    ISBN 978-0-8173-0680-9 (cloth : alk. paper)
    ISBN 978-0-8173-5580-7 (pbk. : alk. paper)
        1. Cotton trade—Florida—Apalachicola—History.  2. Apalachicola
(Fla.)—Economic conditions.  I. Title.
HD9078.A66W55   1993
382′ .41351′0975991—dc20                                          92-28831

To my father,

BROADUS WILLOUGHBY,

and to the memory of his father and grandfather,
successful southern businessmen who taught
their children the value of hard work

# Contents

# Illustrations and Tables

## Maps

## Photographs

## Tables

# *Preface*

I am a "river person" who has spent many days quietly floating down southern waterways. However, until I was hired by an attorney to prove the navigability of one of these rivers, I never appreciated their history. During the course of several years of research in which I attempted to prove that Florida's Peace River had been used for commerce in the antebellum era, I gradually came to the realization that before the advent of improved roads and railways, the various streams of the South had been the region's first superhighways. Naturally, people settled near their sole transportation artery, and river civilizations developed.

I naively decided to write an economic history of one of these river societies, the Apalachicola/Chattahoochee River, even though I was not trained in economic history. As I began sifting through the primary sources, I found much that puzzled me about antebellum business practices. I also found many secondary sources of little help because they were written by economists or economic historians who had written for their peers, using jargon that was often unintelligible to me or making conclusions based on information that was so obvious to them as to not need inclusion but which left the uninitiated scratching her head.

Too often in academia, scholars stake out a small plot as their specialty area and go on to fight rather average turf wars over it. This is unfortunate because general historians and their economically oriented brothers and sisters could learn much from each other by encouraging a fresh perspective. Most historians suffer from "economics anxiety," an illness that causes them to quarantine themselves voluntarily from any mention of the subject. However, in order for the study of history truly to illuminate the past, it must examine all facets of life. I determined there was a need for a primer on the mechanics of the antebellum cotton trade that could be understood by the general public, and I have attempted to fill this need in the following pages.

I am grateful to many for their help in writing this book. Naturally, I would not have gotten far without the advisement of dozens of archivists and librarians. I would particularly like to recognize the following persons whose extraordinary interest and help caused me to find sources that probably would have gone uncovered: William Ervin at Duke University, Anne Gometz at Florida State University, and David Coles at the Florida State Archives. Professors John Lupold and Craig Lloyd of Columbus College were a great help in suggesting sources and in obtaining copies of old photographs.

Jeanne Howard opened her home to me whenever I was in Atlanta and even ran down a few leads for me in the state archives. Niles Schuh generously opened his private collection of Apalachicola letters. Joe Knetsch has liberally shared his discoveries with me. My colleague Jason Silverman read portions of the manuscript, and both he and Lynne Dunn prodded me to finish it in those dark days when I wanted to quit. I owe my little sister Windee and friends Canter Brown and Ginger Williams more than just money for the long-distance bills they each ran up over the months as they also encouraged me not to give up. The editors of *Georgia Historical Quarterly*, *Gulf Coast Historical Review*, and *Florida Historical Quarterly* were supportive as well and have permitted me to reprint portions of previously published articles. I am also grateful to have received financial support from Winthrop College, which awarded me a summer research grant, and the Mrs. Simon Baruch University Award, a grant-in-aid of publication.

Finally, I owe Phillip Ware more than I could ever express here. He caused me to believe in myself as a writer, and his encouragement and criticisms have made me a better one.

Lynn Willoughby
Winthrop University
Rock Hill, S.C.

# Introduction

THE SLEEPY NATION OF THE UNITED STATES AWOKE WITH a start at the dawning of the nineteenth century. Its pulse quickened measurably as it yawned and stretched and began to stir. The acquisition of the Louisiana Purchase of 1803 more than doubled its size in one day, and within only another fifty-odd years its mass would be increased by another 70 percent. Simultaneously, its populace was reproducing quickly and, augmented by immigration, there would be four times as many Americans living on the eve of the Civil War as there had been at century's turn. This young, energetic generation did not remain near its parents' homes on the Atlantic shore either. These people pushed westward, pursuing opportunity, until by 1865, a majority of them would be living west of the original thirteen states.[1]

The invention of the cotton gin in 1793 had created much of this opportunity. Because of this new "engine," growing cotton for export became a viable enterprise. Over the fifty-year period ending in 1860 the amount of cotton produced in America would increase by twenty-two times.[2] No other American export came close to the importance of cotton to the United States economy in the antebellum period. From 1815 to 1860, it alone accounted for over half of the value of domestic exports.[3] In the latter year, earnings from cotton paid for 60 percent of American imports.[4] Like the automobile industry in the next century, the cotton trade's impact rippled over many other segments of the national economy, creating thousands of related jobs. In the shipping industry alone, according to an 1853 congressional report, cotton created seven thousand jobs in river navigation to southern ports. Fifty-five thousand men were engaged in the Gulf and Atlantic coasting trade, and another forty thousand American seamen moved the crop across the Atlantic.[5]

The spread of the Cotton Kingdom into fresh western lands over time dramatically increased production of the staple. But the amount of cotton that could ultimately be produced was dependent on the availability of a market. If a farmer did not have access to a convenient and cheap form of transportation, he was relegated to producing for his own consumption, rather than for the market's. As the population stretched westward, transportation costs became prohibitive, and domestic trade between regions was retarded. Radical changes in transportation were necessary to pull the country along into a nationally integrated capitalist society, and, fortunately for America, transportation was simultaneously undergoing a revolution of its own.[6]

Up to the nineteenth century, overland transportation along paths cut through the wilderness had been prohibitively slow, so trade remained a local phenomenon only. The only viable means of moving products over long distances was by water. Flatboats, drifting downstream, followed the country's natural waterways to markets on the coast or at the juncture of rivers, and, less frequently, these boats were poled or pulled back upstream. By 1807 Robert Fulton had proved the efficacy of using steamboats on eastern rivers, and within ten years western rivers had also adapted to this improved mode of travel. The tempo of American business now accelerated as river travel moved much faster, and two-way traffic became the norm.[7]

But rivers could not take one everywhere one wished to go. Soon visionaries began building canals to link interior areas to the country's riverine network. The most successful such project was the Erie Canal, completed in 1825, which allowed one to travel from the

Great Lakes region of the Midwest to the port of New York via water alone. The success of the canal partly explains why New York became the nation's financial and commercial hub by 1860.[8] Eventually the railroad would further augment the nation's waterways by joining river systems to each other and moving into new areas never serviced by water.

Naturally, as transportation became more reliable, its costs plummeted, and more and more farmers were able to participate in the budding national market economy. Producers of raw and manufactured products could then afford to specialize in what they could most efficiently produce when transportation costs did not prevent them from competing in other regions. Many frontier areas, where farmers had once lived in rural isolation and self-sufficiency, evolved into commercial centers. Yeoman farmers became agri-businessmen.[9]

Although the country was still a long way from having a nationally integrated market, there was ongoing specialization within the regions. The Northeast concentrated on manufacturing; the Northwest specialized in grain and meat production; the South concentrated mostly on cotton for export. Led by the cotton trade, America's domestic commerce grew rapidly so that by 1839 intersectional trade had become more valuable than domestic exports abroad.[10]

Americans were experiencing drastic changes at a remarkable pace. While undergoing the first stages of an industrial revolution, the nation was concurrently going through an agricultural revolution that dramatically increased farm productivity. At the same time, the nation was experiencing a transportation revolution, which picked up the tempo of American business and also brought the various regional markets closer together. Simultaneously, a "commercial revolution" was occurring as well.[11]

Whether agriculturalist or mercantilist, the businessman of the Jacksonian Age was a "Man on the Make." Profit was the all-consuming goal. In the quickly changing business environment opportunity abounded for making money. A new class of entrepreneurs appeared who specialized in marketing and financing the movement of goods. In the cotton trade, factors, brokers, buyers, and warehousemen specialized in buying and selling the crop. Concomitantly, the growing retail trade demanded another group of commercial middlemen, such as commission merchants and storekeepers. Bankers and other financial middlemen were necessary to finance the movement of goods from their place of origin to the marketplace because even though transportation was becoming vastly improved, there was still a lag-time of many weeks or months between production and sale.

During this developmental phase of capitalism, the American economy was as unstable as uranium. Even when the lawmakers felt obliged to attempt some form of regulation of it, they were novices, and much of what they tried failed to bring order to the business environment. Changing conditions and regulations created countless opportunities for the brave-at-heart to venture their capital and credit successfully, but it would take some time before efficient business methods became a matter of custom, instead of one of trial and error. In the meantime, every enterprise was fraught with peril.

The amazing thing about America's early nineteenth-century economy is that it was ultimately triumphant. By the eve of the Civil War, "a commercial revolution had completely transformed the domestic and international trade of the nation."[12] Improved transportation modes had joined the widely dispersed producers to world markets, commercial middlemen had developed efficient means of moving commodities to market, and financial intermediaries tapped foreign money markets in order to finance the entire operation.[13] A sense of order had descended. One purpose of this book is to document this metamorphosis that gradually drew isolated, self-contained local economies into an integrated national market.

The most typical of regional economies in the antebellum period was one based on cotton. This fiber has been called "the most significant single ingredient in the economic life of the whole nation before 1860."[14] If it was that important to the nation as a whole, its impact on the cotton-growing region was nothing short of phenomenal. American cotton production was concentrated in a rather small geographic area. Ninety-five percent of American cotton was produced in only eight southern states.[15] In those states, the very fabric of civilization was woven from cotton fiber, and it is no wonder that a southerner wrote the following in homage: "Great and incalculable is the wondrous power of Cotton! It earns the poor man's bread, and fills the rich man's pocket. It covers new-born infancy, and forms our garmets for the grave. We toil for it by day, and lay ourselves down [with it] by night. . . . The hopes and fears of millions, born and unborn, cluster around those unsightly cotton bales. It permeates through every department of civilized, and it may be, uncivilized life. . . . Wonderful! most wonderful! is the power of cotton! The universe is but a cotton mill, elaborating the necessities of men."[16]

The Cotton South was not monolithic in its development. Instead, it was more a patchwork of separate economies, each developing at its own pace, each based on cotton but reliant on a different river system as its major transportation artery. Because roads in the modern sense did not yet exist to join each river system to each other, each of these river economies within the South could more easily communicate with other regions by salt water than through the forests that separated them. Until other ways were found for traversing the region's dense forests, river transportation was the only viable means of conducting the region's cotton to market. The closer a cotton farmer settled to a navigable river, the easier his life and labor would be. White families, like the Indians who had settled there before them, regarded the river as the nucleus of their civilization.

The Cotton South was blessed with an abundance of these natural highways that linked the ocean with the interior, as far inland as the fall line where navigation was interrupted. The major river systems of the region that flowed into the Gulf of Mexico were the Mississippi, with its port city of New Orleans; the Alabama, which emptied into Mobile Bay; and the Apalachicola/Chattahoochee system, whose port was Apalachicola, Florida. On the Atlantic Coast, the great cotton ports of Savannah and Charleston capitalized on their respective river systems.[17]

In each of these valleys east of the Mississippi River, dynamic river economies developed, each containing the same three elements: a port city on the ocean, minor river trading towns upstream of the port in the coastal plain, and a primary trading center located at the water falls of the piedmont. The muddy river waters linked all components of the local economy together. Thus were joined as symbiotic partners at opposite ends of their respective waterways the markets of Mobile and Montgomery, Alabama; Savannah and Augusta, Georgia; and Apalachicola, Florida, and Columbus, Georgia.

A division of labor existed among the cotton merchants of each local economy. The various tasks necessary to market the crop were divided among upriver merchants and downstream entrepreneurs. Inland cotton factors and commission merchants clustered in the larger communities. They primarily made their fortune in buying plantation supplies for their country clients on credit and selling their cotton on a commission basis when the cotton was harvested. General storekeepers found their niche in the less-populated countryside. They serviced the smaller cotton farmers, who also needed a market for their crop, as well as a source of credit for farm operations throughout the growing season. Coastal factors at the seacoast acted as liaisons between the inland merchants and the cotton buyers who represented mill owners or speculators in such "foreign" markets as New York or London.

Most studies of the United States cotton trade center around the relationship between inland merchants and their planter and farmer clients. These studies include in their account the interaction between upcountry businessmen and coastal merchants, but only peripherally and from an upriver perspective. By concentrating on the freshwater end of the cotton trade, the explanation of America's cotton marketing structure remains half-told.

The cotton trade network stretched from the pine forests of the southern frontier up America's eastern shore to the port of New York or the mills of New England and across the Atlantic Ocean to the money and cotton markets of Europe. The southern coastal merchant sat in the center of these convergent maritime routes, providing marketing services to clients upriver only by exploiting his connections in the North or England.

Therefore, in order to explain more fully the international cotton marketing structure, this book will center on one of the South's cotton ports, Apalachicola, Florida. Although the port's relationship to the river hinterland is examined in detail, I do not wish to end my examination of the antebellum cotton marketing system at the Gulf of Mexico. Apalachicola represented a crucial connection between South and North, America and Europe, in this important international trade.

This trade followed a route of least resistance. That is, trade flowed from one place to another because it made economic sense to do so. Summary figures published in contemporary commercial newspapers that reported the number of cotton bales received in a port like Apalachicola and to which port they were destined stop short of explaining why trade patterns developed as they did. However, cataloging the movements and outbound cargo of the fleet of vessels that called on Apalachicola will provide important clues about the nature of trade flows and the interrelationship among all the cotton ports. Furthermore, a study of Apalachicola imports will indicate the economic health and character of the entire river valley.

After describing Apalachicola's nexus within the international cotton trade, an examination of the business environment of this individual river economy is necessary. A critique of the money and banking conditions within this economy provides the economic setting necessary to gain an appreciation of the complications unknown to modern businessmen that antebellum entrepreneurs faced daily and helps to explain the peculiarities of antebellum business customs.

The men who made their living in the cotton trade adapted to the financial conditions of the river valley as best they could. Some became wealthy; many more were broken by them, but they all followed similar daily routines, formed partnerships rather casually by modern standards, and maintained friendships and rivalries among their competitors. The interaction of the various cotton men both upriver and at the seaport is also a theme of this book.

Particularly at Apalachicola, Yankees dominated the cotton market. While extant sources do not tell us in what ways the northerners might have influenced southern business styles, it is obvious that southern social values did influence many of these northerners and that animosity toward the Yankees predated the Civil War.

Despite the rivalry and competition among the cotton merchants of the river valley, they were able to work cooperatively enough to move the commodity efficiently out of the South to its place of consumption. However, the order of this economic unit was not permanent. The coming of the railroad shattered the old business organization by creating new avenues of commerce, and once this change occurred the river valley would never again be the intact and isolated economic unit of the past. Transportation and communications not only moved more quickly in the new age but also moved in new directions. As rail lines were built to connect or circumvent the river systems, the preeminence of river transportation was mortally challenged.

When geographical features no longer solely determined the location of trading centers, a new phase of competition was born. The city leaders who triumphed in this new scramble for market shares were the aggressive ones who wagered their own money on the effectiveness of the iron horse and won their bet. As we will see, the merchants of Columbus, Georgia, at the northern end of the Apalachicola/Chattahoochee River somewhat reluctantly joined this group of winners, and the city continued to grow while the seaport of Apalachicola allowed time to pass it by.

Every local river economy possessed its own distinctiveness. The differences among them were affected by the character of the various rivers themselves, as well as by the people who settled there. The business setting of the Apalachicola/Chattahoochee River valley was also shaded by its distinct set of banking and monetary conditions. Economic conditions, while similar throughout the South, varied from state to state since each one's legislature approached economic development in its own way. The young Apalachicola/Chattahoochee River valley was hindered by its location amid three different states, each operating at different developmental stages and devising disparate fiscal policies. No other southeastern river valley had to contend with this complication. For that reason this study will give us insight into some of the variations among the many river-centered economies of the South.

However, regardless of the disparities in character among the various river economies, they were all connected by the Atlantic Ocean to the same nucleus. English mills were the largest consumers of American cotton, and English import houses (usually with New York branch offices) dominated the financing of the trade. This relatively small number of firms directly or indirectly dictated business procedures to virtually all coastal merchants, and uniformity in business practices was rapidly accomplished. Because these practices were reflected in the cinnamon-tinted waters of the Apalachicola/Chattahoochee River, a study of this valley's antebellum business customs serves as a microcosm of the mechanics of the entire South's cotton trade.

# 1

## A Cotton Economy

HE PORT CITY OF APALACHICOLA, FLORIDA, ON THE Gulf of Mexico exported its first bale of cotton in 1822.[1] The future of this small port held promise. The city lay at the mouth of "the largest and longest river system in the southeastern United States."[2] This waterway (composed of the Chipola and the Apalachicola rivers in Florida and the Chattahoochee and Flint rivers in Georgia and Alabama) dissected rich cotton lands only then being opened for white settlement as the Creek Indians were pushed out of their homelands.

The region was a frontier in its truest sense. Florida did not become a United States possession until 1821 or a state until 1845. As late as 1840 the Apalachicola newspaper reported sporadic Indian attacks on the valley's newcomers.[3] As the Indians were gradually forced off their lands, eager white cotton farmers moved in quickly to claim it, to clear away the pine trees, and to plant the seeds that they believed would make them wealthy in the rich red earth.

Apalachicola, first called "West Point," was incorporated in 1829. By 1836 fifty thousand bales of cotton were being exported from there, and it had become the third largest cotton port on the Gulf of Mexico behind New Orleans and Mobile. By 1840 forty-three im-

posing brick and granite cotton warehouses guarded Apalachicola's
river bank, each thirty feet wide and three stories tall.[4]

As the port grew, it faced a competitor from the west. The town
of St. Joseph, Florida, was created for the sole purpose of stealing
Apalachicola's cotton trade. A railroad (Florida's first) was built
from Iola, on the Apalachicola River, to St. Joseph, on the Gulf of
Mexico, in order to bypass the older port. The railroad was completed in 1839, and for a couple of years the upstart gave Apalachicola a run for its money, but a yellow fever epidemic in 1841
was so deadly that the town was abandoned, leaving Apalachicola as
the sole recipient of the river trade. The decade of the 1840s would
prove to be Apalachicola's golden years.[5]

The city's year-round residents numbered only around one thousand, but in the cotton marketing season, which was at its peak
between December and April, the population multipled several-
fold.[6] The winter populace was a cosmopolitan lot of mostly northerners and foreigners who came there for the sole purpose of making
their fortunes in cotton. When the summer breezes brought the
mosquitoes and the heat, they were gone again to their homes in
more healthful climes. In addition to the businessmen, thousands of
seamen from all over the world also thronged the waterfront during
the busy season,[7] thus adding to the congestion of the streets already obstructed with cotton bales and bustling with activity.

Apalachicola was a flurry of activity during the commercial season. Hundreds of bales of cotton spilled out of the warehouses and
clogged the streets. The auction bell clanged as draymen rushed the
bales from the wharves to the compresses to the warehouses and
back again. Cotton factors, whose job it was to sell the cotton, held
court in their counting rooms on the second floor of their warehouses. Here they laid out samples for prospective buyers, and they
dashed off letters to their associates in New York and Europe noti-
fying them of an ensuing shipment. They arranged for the bales to
be mended or repacked, insured, and stored. They dickered over
the lowest ocean freightage, and they arranged financing so that
neither they nor their clients had to wait for the cotton to reach the
English textile mill before they received compensation. They sent

other letters upriver to the farmer who waited to hear what his year's labor would bring. All day long their clerks bent over the precious accounting books that brought order to the entire operation. Long into the night, lamplights glowed from the upstairs windows of the counting rooms on Water Street.

These people were as obsessed with the staple as were their counterparts in Mobile, where one visitor claimed: "people live in cotton houses and ride in cotton carriages. They buy cotton, sell cotton, think cotton, eat cotton, drink cotton, and dream cotton. They marry cotton wives, and unto them are born cotton children. In enumerating the charms of a fair widow, they begin by saying she makes so many bales of cotton. It is the great staple, the sum and substance of Alabama."[8]

A resident of Apalachicola during its preeminence as a cotton port later recalled that he had enjoyed the heady days there when money was easy, "[w]ater was scacer [sic] than champagne, and jolly good fellows were plentiful as blackberries."[9] This was not just the opinion of one man. A northerner who worked several cotton seasons in Apalachicola reported that even though the place had its drawbacks, the port abounded in good food and "mighty good liquors" and "plenty of fellows that will eat & drink with [you] night & day."[10]

But the summer off-season was another matter. The town virtually closed down. Steamboats no longer jockeyed for their place at the wharves. Businesses closed. The streets became deserted. Those few who did remain in town, "seemed to drag along as though each step were the effort of an involuntary struggle. . . . Everything was quiet, quiet, quiet, and but for 'dame fashion,' 'bustle' would have become an obsolete idea."[11]

The pulse of this community was quieted or quickened according to the state of its major artery, the river. The waterway originated as two Georgia streams, the Chattahoochee and the Flint rivers, which flowed from north Georgia in a southwesterly direction roughly paralleling each other through southwest Georgia until they converged at the Florida and Alabama boundaries. From this point of their confluence to where the waters reached the Gulf of Mexico, the river was known as the Apalachicola. In Florida a smaller stream known as the Chipola originated west of the larger course near the Alabama line and paralleled the Apalachicola for about fifty miles before the two united and wound their way to the Gulf.

The river was the highway that linked the port with the rich cotton fields of Georgia and Alabama and, beyond them, the industrial and commercial city of Columbus, Georgia. Until the railroads came in from east and west to break up this unit in the 1850s, residents throughout the valley seemed to face inward toward the river that would take the cotton to market or mill. It was not a perfect transportation network. In the dry summer months the streams dwindled to a thread, carrying less than two feet of water in many places. Every summer commerce halted until the river again resumed its usable state.

Fortunately for those involved in the cotton trade, the rise of the river generally coincided with the harvest of cotton. Planters usually began picking cotton in August. After the cotton was ginned to remove its seeds and compressed into bales, growers could store the nonperishable bales on their farms indefinitely until the river was capable of transporting the crop to market. Generally the Apalachicola/Chattahoochee River system became boatable by Christmas and remained so until May or June.

Many bales of cotton passed through the port of Apalachicola during this short business season. Total cotton receipts there generally increased in the 1840s from a low of about 55,000 bales in 1840 to around 140,000 in 1853.[12] Railroad incursion into the valley in the latter year siphoned off cotton to other ports, but a surge in general cotton production in the late 1850s compensated for the cotton Apalachicola lost to Savannah and Mobile, and by 1860 receipts had again climbed to over 130,000 bales.[13]

Most of Apalachicola's cotton was destined for Liverpool, England, the seaport of the great Manchester textile mills. One quarter of the cotton that eventually reached England was detoured through New York, which needed southern cotton to fill the holds of its Europe-bound packets. Southern cotton dealers also needed New York to provide financial backing for its shipments to England.

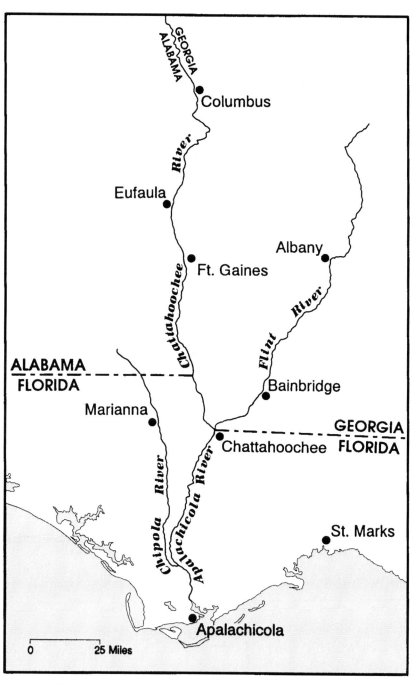

The Apalachicola/Chattahoochee River Valley

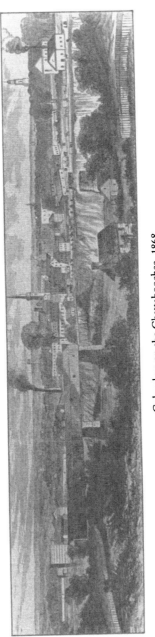

Columbus on the Chattahoochee, 1868
(Columbus College Archives)

Apalachicola cotton dealers also shipped regularly to Havre, France; Providence, Rhode Island; Boston; and Baltimore.[14]

Apalachicola was not the only cotton market on the river. At the opposite end of the river stood Columbus, Georgia. Laid out in 1828 for speculative purposes as soon as Georgia received legal claim to this land from the Creek Indians, it quickly became "the boom town of west Georgia."[15] For many years, Columbus perched on the western edge of "civilization," for Indians continued to hold onto their lands on the Alabama side of the Chattahoochee throughout most of the 1830s.[16] As late as 1844 one traveler learned that the settlement across the river (modern-day Phenix City, Alabama) had been nicknamed "Sodom" because of the rough crowd that assembled there.[17] Columbus itself was a bawdy town where liquor flowed and the druggist proudly displayed the latest models of stilettos.[18] It was a town of dichotomies; some travelers remarked on its dirty run-down hotels,[19] while others were taken with its natural beauty.[20]

Regardless of its origins, Columbus soon became one of the major commercial centers of Georgia. Located at the fall line, the town lay at the head of navigation of the Chattahoochee River. Paths cut into the forest in all directions allowed those farmers living within a day's ride to haul their cotton by wagon into the city where steamboats waited at the docks to carry the staple to the coast. Many local farmers found Columbus to be a convenient market for both selling their cotton and buying their supplies, and a brisk "wagon trade" developed there.

During the fall and winter months the crude roads that stretched out from the city conducted wagon after wagon loaded with cotton from the surrounding fields. By 1845 the city's population, numbering almost five thousand, greatly outnumbered that of Apalachicola. It boasted two hundred businesses including twenty-six drygoods stores, fifty-seven provisions stores, and five cotton warehouses. Yearly cotton receipts in Columbus from 1840 to 1855 averaged about seventy thousand bales, and over 100,000 after 1855.[21]

Columbus was primarily a cotton marketing center, but it was more diversified than its sibling city at the Gulf. Apparently the men of capital in Columbus were more willing to put their money into manufacturing enterprises than were their counterparts in most areas of the South.[22] By 1849 five textile factories used the water power provided by Columbus's breathtakingly beautiful falls to spin local cotton into yarn and shirting. There was also a paper mill, a flour- and gristmill, two foundries, a machine shop, and a factory that made cotton gins.[23]

By 1860 Columbus had a population of nine thousand.[24] In textile production, it was second only to Richmond in the South.[25] Those businesses advertising that year included six banking institutions, seven cotton commission businesses, and eight cotton brokers. Forty-six groceries served the thriving wagon trade.[26]

Both Columbus and Apalachicola owed their existence to the hinterland lying between them. The triangles of land between the Flint and Chattahoochee rivers in Georgia and the Chipola and Apalachicola rivers in Florida were prime cotton lands, and the area, once opened to whites, was settled rapidly. By 1840 the population of those Georgia counties lying between the Flint and Chattahoochee rivers below the fall line was almost ninety thousand.[27] Ten years later there were 185,000 people living in the entire river valley.[28]

As the white population increased, lesser trading towns sprouted along the riverbanks. Eufaula, Alabama, located about forty-five miles below Columbus on the Chattahoochee, was another significant regional cotton market, for it often served as the head of navigation during the dry summer months. Like Columbus, it began as a raucous frontier town built on the foundation of a Creek Indian town. White cotton farmers had been so eager to begin cultivating this land that they had not even paused to purchase it first, precipitating a local war.[29]

Albany, Georgia, at the head of navigation of the Flint River, was an important trade center for the forwarding of cotton to the Gulf by barges, as well as for the ancillary grocery trade. Marianna, Florida, at the head of navigation of the Chipola River was another. Scores of minor markets were situated all along the river system wherever individuals built steamboat landings and waterside warehouses.

On the Alabama side of the river, there was a brisk wagon trade at Otho, Abbeville, Columbia, Franklin, and Seale.[30] In Georgia there were markets at Fort Gaines on the Chattahoochee and Bainbridge on the lower Flint, but almost every boat landing had a warehouse and resident entrepreneur.[31] There were twenty-five landings on the Apalachicola and Chattahoochee rivers between Apalachicola and Columbus.[32]

In the lonely pine forests of Georgia, Alabama, and north Florida, these wharves served as gathering places for farmers and planters, travelers, and occasionally the idle daughters of nearby plantations. The sporadic arrival of a steamboat, announced by the blast of a whistle or the firing of a gun, brought people scurrying toward the landing to watch the slaves load and unload the steamboat. Since many of these landings were located on steep bluffs, this process was quite interesting to observe. Long wooden slides, which extended from the top of the bluff to the river's edge, were used to conduct the cargo down the hill. Bale after bale of cotton, as well as other heavy freight (even pigs), were sent tumbling down the steep incline and into the bowels of the boat. When at last the freight was stored and the shouting had stopped, the steamer noisily pulled away from the dock and disappeared around the bend in a cloud of smoke, leaving the onlookers to return to the relative quiet and isolation of their work until the next steamer announced itself.[33]

Many men made their living executing the various specialized tasks necessary in moving the cotton from field to mill. As one way of distinguishing them from each other, cotton merchants can be classified as being either buyers or sellers. Cotton factors were paid a commission of 2.5 percent by the grower to *sell* his cotton. Although the farmer retained ownership of the staple, the factor acted in his own name. The rationale for this custom was that the factor had incurred expenses in transporting and storing the cotton before sale and had usually given the grower a partial payment in advance of the sale. Therefore, he acquired a lien on the cotton "which gave him the right to deal with it in a manner that would protect his acquired interest."[34]

Commission merchants were paid a commission of 2.5 percent for *buying* commodities for someone else. Eventually the terms *factor* and *commission merchant* were used interchangeably (as they are throughout this book) because the same man charged with selling a planter's cotton at harvesttime was usually also the one who had bought plantation supplies for the grower throughout the season, carrying the debit on his books until the cotton sale compensated him.

However, in the 1840s businessmen were more likely than any other time to use the terms literally. For example, the officers in the firm of Flewellen and Butt of Apalachicola called themselves "Factors and Commission Merchants" in their advertisements, saying, "we shall be sellers, not buyers of Cotton; and will give prompt attention to the filling of all orders for Bagging, Rope, Family supplies, etc."[35] Likewise, Sims and Cheever of Albany, Georgia, who also specialized in buying cotton and purchasing supplies on commission, referred to themselves as "Factors and General Commission Merchants" in their advertising.[36]

This distinction made between factors and commission merchants was particularly necessary in Apalachicola, for there existed a marked division of labor within the port. In addition to the factors who sold cotton, there was a large class of merchants who bought cotton on commission for northern and European concerns. Indeed, a contemporary commented in 1845 that the Apalachicola market was controlled by those working for northern manufacturers.[37]

Commission merchants retained to buy cotton, rather than to sell it, have generally been ignored by southern economic historians. Norman Sydney Buck wrote in 1925 that there may exist a "separate class of buying factors," but he found he did not have enough evidence to make a conclusion.[38] No one since his study has mentioned American "buying factors." However, at least eight different Apalachicola firms acted as commission merchants for New England textile mills alone.[39] L. F. E. Dugas of Apalachicola worked solely as a commission merchant, buying cotton for commission houses in New York, France, and Charleston. For his efforts he received 2.5 percent of the gross amount of the sale.[40]

However, even in the 1840s, the literal distinction between commission merchants and factors as buyers or sellers was usually not made. In most advertisements, the terms were used interchangeably. For example, whereas M. M. Butt and E. R. Flewellen in Apalachicola advertised as being "Factors and Commission Merchants" in 1843, the previous year Butt was involved in another partnership that referred to themselves as "Commission Merchants" but who paid "particular attention" to "*selling* Cotton."[41] Furthermore, "commission merchant" P. A. Clayton advertised that he would take orders to *buy or sell* cotton. By the 1850s it was rare to see the term "factor" used at all.[42]

Whatever the appellation used, the job of selling cotton on commission was multifaceted. The factor's primary task was to find a buyer for the planter's cotton, but in order to do that he first had to evaluate the cotton, repackage it, and store it. Once it was in a warehouse the factor studied the returns of all the American and foreign markets to determine trends in the price of the staple and in which market he should sell the cotton. If the product was not sold locally, he had to engage a ship at a cost that would not devour the profits of the final sale.

Most importantly the factor had to arrange financing. The planter expected an advance equal to one-half to three-fourths of the value of his cotton. This money did not come directly from the factor, but from the buyer. The financial chain was a long and torturous one involving a series of advances, the number of which corresponding to the number of middlemen. The factor spent most of his workday in keeping books. He noted not only the future of each cotton bale but also the other debits made to the planter's account. During the growing season the planter charged clothing, groceries, and tools and often borrowed money from the factor. The entire account was settled at the end of the cotton season when the crop had finally been sold.

In order to be able to account for each bale of cotton as it moved from grower to middleman to mill, it was necessary for each to retain a separate identity. Each planter branded his bales using a successive numbering system coupled usually with his initials. Then, as the cotton moved downriver and overseas, it was referred to in the paperwork by this label. Bills of lading, warehouse receipts, and bills of sale all listed each bale by name.

One of the first skills a cotton factor learned was how to sample and grade cotton. To determine the quality of the product he thrust a gimlet into the bale. The serrated sides of this instrument cut out a small handful of cotton that was then examined to determine its quality.[43]

Color, length of staple, and the amount of foreign matter in the sample determined its classification. The most preferred cotton had a creamy tint, which farmers could effect by storing the cotton for some time before ginning so that the oil from the seed exuded into the fiber.[44] Dull white cotton was less desirable, but it was much more preferred than "spotted" or "tinged" cotton that had a brown discoloration caused by frost or boll weevil damage. A grayish tint to the cotton indicated it had been exposed too long to rain, fog, or dust.[45]

The color and the length of the staple (the longer, the more valuable it was) together with an assessment of how much trash was thrown into the gin determined to which of thirteen distinct grades of cotton the bale belonged. These standard grades (in descending order) were:

| | |
|---|---|
| Fair | Middling |
| Strict middling fair | Strict low middling |
| Middling fair | Low middling |
| Strict good middling | Strict good ordinary |
| Good middling | Good ordinary |
| Strict middling | Strict ordinary |
| | Ordinary[46] |

Middling cotton was the basic grade from which all other classifications were figured.[47] It was said that if for every pound of clean cotton the gin threw in the fragments of one dead leaf, the grade would be good middling. The equivalent of two leaves per pound produced a classification of strict middling and so on.[48]

After samples were taken, the cotton factor wrote the planter to inform him how the cotton had been classified and what the prospects were for that grade in both local and foreign markets. William G. Porter and Company wrote this typical advisement to a client in 1859: "We put the samples on the boards to day and in a more careful examination find we were mistaken when we valued the crop at 10½ to 10⅝ [cents per pound] in our last. The crops from the neighbourhood of your plantation appear to have been injured by the storm in Sept. [T]hey are dingy in color and more trashy than usual."[49]

Besides the grade of a bale of cotton, its port city also affected its sale price. Apalachicola cotton was more prized than the Georgia upland variety marketed through Savannah or Charleston.[50] It was said that cotton of the same grade sold for from ¼ to ⅜ cent higher in the Apalachicola market than in Savannah simply because of its reputation for quality because, "It is the *port* as well as the *quality* that gives character to cotton."[51]

The cotton factor and the planter had a symbiotic business relationship. The grower needed the merchant to extend credit and to market his cotton while he concentrated his resources on raising as much cotton as possible. The factor made his income by charging a fee for each of the services he provided. Like their counterparts in Mobile, Apalachicola factors charged 2.5 percent for selling cotton and buying merchandise. They also charged brokerage fees for negotiating loans, procuring bills of exchange, and discounting promissory notes.[52]

Relations between planters and their factors were, for the most part, warm and trusting. However, there were occasions when the planter felt he had been cheated in the sale of his cotton as did the brother of Alexander Allen of Bainbridge, Georgia, whom Allen wrote to say, "I sympathize with you in the unfortunate sale of your cotton. There must be some rascality in the matter. Have it investigated."[53]

There was certainly opportunity for distant factors to cheat their clients, but most planters had access to enough market information to keep the factors honest. Many growers subscribed to agricultural or commercial journals that published (albeit belatedly) the going price of cotton in the various markets. Because the planters knew approximately when their cotton arrived in the market, they could determine what their cotton should have brought.[54]

Planters had a natural distrust for the middlemen. From their standpoint it seemed there was abundant profit to be made in cotton factorage. The commission, freightage, finance, and other charges added to the cost of a bale of cotton sold overseas could total as much as 40 percent of the original value of the cotton.[55] When sold locally and financing was not involved, the costs of freight to Apalachicola, wharfage, weighing, insurance, storage, sampling, drayage, mending, and selling equaled about 8 percent.[56] Most of this amount, however, did not represent profit for the commission merchant who simply passed his costs on to the planter.

Southern cotton merchants had their own complaints about the planters. Their major grievance was that they used fraudulent methods in packing their cotton into bales. Occasionally planters placed stones inside the bales or poured water into them to make them heavier. Often two or more grades were packed together with the inferior quality placed on the inside, safely out of reach of the sampler's gimlet.[57]

In Apalachicola's case it seems most mixed cotton bales were not the result of intentional fraud but rather the result of careless packing. A letter from an Apalachicola factor to a Flint River planter explained the problem: "This habit of mixing cotton arises from ginning as long as possible and delaying the packing for rainy days. The poor and good cotton is ginned separately, but all trod down in the lint room until it can hold no more, and then packed without separating the qualities."[58]

In the long run, negligent planters were only hurting themselves. When a bale of mixed cotton reached the English or northern manufacturer it was rejected because one staple length could not be substituted for another in spinning the fiber into yarn.[59] The cotton was then thrown back on the merchant who had to remarket it as mixed cotton. A mixed bale seldom brought more than the market value of the lowest grade. If the practice became habitual, buyers might become prejudiced against the cotton of a certain factor or port.[60]

In addition to those who made their living in buying or selling cotton on commission, there were others directly involved in the cotton trade. "Buyers" worked exclusively as agents for foreign textile mills or commission houses. These men received very strict instructions from their employer as to how much to buy, of what grade, and at what price. The Columbus firm of Hall and DeBlois was agent for a group of Lowell, Massachusetts, textile companies, and its warehouse was known by everyone as the "Lowell Warehouse."[61]

Samuel Cassin, an Englishman at Apalachicola, was the agent of the related commission firms of Brown Brothers and Company of New York and Brown, Shipley and Company of Liverpool. These two firms paid Cassin 1 percent commission to purchase cotton on their account from other commission merchants in the river valley who also received a percentage of the gross sale equaling from .5 to 1 percent.[62] Cassin's fee was naturally less than the standard charged by commission merchants because he was not doing business in his own name and, therefore, risked nothing personally. The fee paid to resident commission merchants by him was probably a brokerage fee charged for bringing buyer and seller together.

In addition to those buyers who labored on behalf of another's account, speculators bought cotton in their own name with the intention of buying low and selling high. Oliver Tillinghast of Columbus was a true speculator. On his first enterprise he borrowed money to buy cotton outright, then after much trouble and expense managed to charter an oceangoer to transport it from Apalachicola to Liverpool. This was a high risk business that should have been left to those who had money to lose.[63]

After a poor start Tillinghast confined his business to buying and selling locally in the Columbus market. In 1845 he did well, but the next year he "worked hard all the season and made nothing."[64] By 1852 it appeared he had become more cautious, and was then "brokering" cotton in Columbus for account of the Apalachicola firm of Nourse, Stone and Company.[65] In actuality he was working off some old loans made with the coastal factors by applying his commissions for buying cotton for the Floridians toward his debts with them.[66] However, two years later his father complained he was back "in the city, working hard, for what I fear will pay him but little—buying cotton."[67]

Everyone associated even remotely with the cotton trade was constantly tempted to speculate in it. One man commented in 1845, "It seems as if the Cotton trade was never to be governed by the same commonsense rules that prevail in other commercial transactions, [sic] there seems to be a charm in the great southern staple that leads people out of their sober senses."[68] Paris Tillinghast, owner of a Columbus mercantile store, dabbled in cotton speculation on the side. Like his son Oliver, he found that these enterprises rarely came out in the black, yet he continued to speculate.[69]

Commission merchants were especially tempted to buy cotton on their own account even though this activity was in direct conflict with their primary obligation to sell the planter's cotton at the highest price attainable. Advertisements by two Columbus firms vowing not to speculate in cotton intimate that the practice was viewed as both unprincipled and prevalent.[70]

Other cotton buyers located in the countryside were not speculators but general storekeepers who offered drygoods, equipment, and food on credit to the smaller grower who paid for these necessaries with cotton at the end of the growing season. Once the country storekeeper's warehouse was full of cotton he sold it to a buyer or consigned it to a factor to sell. In this way the many small producers in the valley found access to the commercial market, and the smaller merchants became preferred customers of the commission merchants. Inasmuch as 60 percent of the growers of this region had farms of less than one hundred acres in 1860, the country storekeepers were a vital cog in the cotton-marketing machinery.[71]

The country store owner's relationship with the small farmer corresponded to that between the commission merchant and the large planter. Like the commission merchant in the larger towns, the country storekeeper extended credit to the farmer who paid for it with his cotton. The difference between the country storekeeper and the commission merchant was one of proportions. The general storekeeper had hundreds of small accounts while the commission merchant had relatively few but larger ones. The farmer produced a smaller crop, therefore his credit needs were more modest, but he nevertheless needed long-term credit as much as the planter did.[72]

Country storekeepers provided a much-needed service to the farmers whom the commission merchants perceived as being a less attractive investment risk. Farmers were less desirable clients than planters, because planters required a larger volume of supplies throughout the year, and they were more restricted to raising cotton year after year. Farmers could more easily move to new lands or, during a depression, switch to producing foodstuffs than planters who had to produce even more of a cash crop to offset declining prices.[73]

The firm of Copeland and Cannon in Eufaula, Alabama, held scores of accounts with local farmers that usually amounted to no more than one hundred dollars each. The merchants extended small amounts of credit and groceries to the farmers who repaid the debts with several bales of cotton at harvest time. The only cash that passed hands was paid to balance the account at the end of the year.[74]

A farmer in Henry County, Alabama, had accounts like the above with William Mount and Company in Franklin, Alabama, and A. C. Gordon and Company.[75] John Dill and Company in Fort Gaines, Georgia, on the banks of the Chattahoochee, accepted cotton in amounts of as little as one dollar's worth as well as "sundries," which were probably other farm produce. The firms paid cash to settle the accounts at the end of the cotton season around May of each year.[76]

Although much less is known about them, another class of cotton merchant was the broker. Brokers were employed as intermediaries between buyer and seller. When a buyer could not find the price or grade of cotton he wanted readily in the open market, or he simply did not wish to spend his time in searching for it, he could employ a broker who did the footwork for him. The broker's task was to find a person willing to sell at the specifications of the buyer.

Whereas factors actually took possession of the cotton and made contracts in their own name, which were binding on the planter (who actually owned the cotton), brokers did not. The latter were paid a commission of .5 to 1 percent in every gulf port for bringing the buyer and seller together.[77] Because their risk was less than the factor or commission merchant, who advanced money to the owner before the sale, brokers' commissions were less.[78]

Very little is known about the brokers in Apalachicola and their significance in the cotton market. In only one year did cotton brokers advertise locally, and in that case there were only three who did so.[79] They seem to have had a bigger presence in Columbus where twelve were listed as doing business there in 1859.[80]

In addition to the buyers, brokers, and commission merchants, many other people found related work in the cotton trade. Forwarding merchants did not buy or sell, but specialized in overseeing the transfer of the bales from one form of conveyance to another. Apalachicola forwarding merchants received cotton from the river steamboats that docked there, then arranged ocean transportation for it. In the meantime, they often had the cotton stored. In return for their labors they received a fee of about fifty cents per bale in addition to being reimbursed for any costs they incurred such as storage and drayage.[81]

Columbus factors often engaged Apalachicola firms to forward their cotton for them. At the beginning of the 1838 season, one merchant in Apalachicola commented that almost all of the 2,500 bales received thus far in the port had been forwarded "for acct. of the Columbus Merchants."[82]

Shipping merchants in Apalachicola worked on behalf of ship owners. They advertised in the local newspaper the availability of the vessel, its destination, and its approximate sailing date. Their task was to fill the hold of the ship with cargo at the highest freightage possible while taking as little time as possible in doing so. To encourage large consignments, they gave volume discounts.[83]

Warehouse owners throughout the valley stored cotton until it was sold or shipped elsewhere. They usually received twelve and one-half cents per bale for the first month and six and one-half cents per month thereafter, or they might charge twenty-five cents "for the season."[84]

In both Columbus and Apalachicola men specialized in compressing the cotton to ready it for transport. When cotton arrived from the farm, it was either in the form of "round bales," that were tubular pieces of bagging that had been filled by tramping the cotton into it, or "square bales" covered with bagging that had been compressed first by "foot labor" and then with a large wooden screw. The plantation presses were not sufficiently strong to compress the bales for export, and by the time they reached the coast they were in poor condition. Before the cotton left Apalachicola it had to be recompressed into a smaller parcel by using steam or hydraulic power.[85]

In 1843 there were both screw and hydraulic presses in the port. They each charged more for cotton bound to Europe than coastwise, for traveling the longer distance required more preparation.[86] By 1850 all four of the presses in town were steam-powered. Together they employed 111 hands and represented an investment of eighty-five thousand dollars.[87]

Another occupation essential to the cotton trade was that of cotton weigher. To ensure the integrity of Apalachicola merchants and their cotton, weighers were appointed first by the Apalachicola city council and, upon Florida's statehood, by the governor.[88] It was illegal to have one's cotton weighed by anyone other than an official weigher, but there were usually from six to eight to choose from.[89]

Apparently competition among them was steep, and one weigher solicited the merchants' business by having the following published: "He has a family dependent on his labor, and hopes that opportunity will be afforded him to gain a support for them in this community, where such an appeal has never been made in vain."[90]

Insurance agents covered the likely risk of fire while the cotton was being transported and stored. Cotton was an extremely combustible material, and fires in warehouses and on steamboats were a common occurrence. Most of the insurance companies operating in this region were based in New York or Hartford, Connecticut. Aetna, New York Equitable, and the Protection Insurance Company of Hartford all had offices in both Apalachicola and Columbus.[91] Typically, insurance advertisements offered to insure cotton "in Warehouses, Sheds, Presses, or on the Wharf."[92]

Loss at sea was another risk handled by Apalachicola agents. Occasionally, marine insurance was used as a means to hedge against a falling cotton market. For example, a New York commission firm informed a Marianna farmer that the ship carrying his cotton to the North was fully due but had not yet arrived. The firm consoled him by saying the cotton was well insured and "if she does not arrive you will [be] better off than you will be if She comes in."[93]

Both bankers and lawyers were also necessary to the cotton trade. Financiers were needed to provide credit to the cotton men. Their role will be discussed in detail in chapter five. Lawyers spent a large proportion of their time acting as collectors of overdue debts. They advertised in local newspapers that they would attend to claims against anyone living in the adjoining countryside,[94] and received in return a lucrative fee.[95] Attorneys also provided confidential credit information on local businessmen to foreign credit-rating agencies at no charge in exchange for receiving their collecting business.[96]

Informants of the credit-rating agency, R. G. Dun and Company, the forerunner of Dun and Bradstreet, operated throughout the river valley. Every few years, these people collected personal information on the merchants such as their net worth, the nature of their business, and their character. These agents described Apalachicola cotton factors variously as everything from "drinks like a fish" or "an unmitigated rascal" to "prudent money making man" and "good for all his contracts."[97] Unfortunately for those receiving a negative recommendation, this information was highly subjective and often based on hearsay, but prospective northern creditors of these entrepreneurs had little other means of determining whether their money would be safe.

Directly or indirectly, virtually everyone in the river valley made their living from cotton. Be they grocers supplying plantation supplies or steamboat captains providing transportation and communications within the valley, each entrepreneur filled a niche in this cotton monoculture. Like their counterparts in the Alabama and Mississippi River systems to the west and the Savannah to the east, growing, buying, and selling cotton were the major preoccupations.

Indeed, in the mind of each valley's entrepreneurs, the status of the cotton crop very nearly approached that of an obsession.

Together the many occupations associated with the cotton trade of the Apalachicola/Chattahoochee River valley formed a practical marketing network and gave order to this economic system whose boundaries paralleled the river's edge. It was the river that tied all parts of this local economy together. Until the railroads pierced the valley from east and west to challenge the supremacy of these waters, this economic unit would remain isolated, yet intact.

# 2

## *Apalachicola Aweigh*

IKE A LOCKET TIED TO THE END OF A TANGLED BROWN ribbon, the port of Apalachicola adorned the long and twisting river. Only via the Apalachicola/Chattahoochee River was the seaport joined to the cotton fields and communities to its north. But poised on the edge of the Gulf of Mexico, the city rarely perceived its isolation. Populated largely by northerners and visited frequently by seafarers from the world over, Apalachicola had a cosmopolitan charm.

The city was at its finest at dawn, and one could best view daybreak from the city wharf on the west bank of the Apalachicola River just north of where it empties into the bay. Standing with one's back to the city's commercial district and looking eastward beyond the steamboats that crowded the dock, one glimpsed the wide Apalachicola estuary that reflected the rosy brightness of the early morning sky. Gazing southward one beheld the vast Apalachicola Bay, or St. George Sound, extending seven miles across at its widest point and thirty-eight miles east to west. Silhouetted against the rising sun, dozens of sailboats strained against their anchor lines, pointing out the prevailing breeze or tide. On the southern horizon lay long and narrow, alligator-infested St. George Island, which, along with Dog Island to its east and St. Vincent

Island to its west, stood sentinel against the often turbulent seas of the Gulf of Mexico.

To enter the sound from the Gulf, nineteenth-century sailors used either West Pass between St. Vincent's and St. George's or East Pass between St. George's and Dog Island. Lighthouses located at the western ends of both St. George's and Dog Island marked the accesses. From offshore, seamen had little trouble distinguishing between the passes after dark. In the entire North Florida Gulf Coast there were only five lights, and of the two demarcating Apalachicola's harbor, the westernmost's yellow beam shone intermittently while the red beacon at East Pass burned uninterruptedly.[1] Once in sight of the passes, the larger vessels entering the bay required a harbor pilot to steer the craft safely to their moorings just inside the sound and several miles from town.[2] Only the shallow-draft boats could pass over the sandbar near the mouth of the river in order to reach the municipal wharf.

Those sailors who were lucky enough to pull shore leave found a lively place in which to exercise their sea legs, considering the size of the population.[3] There were bars, hotels, oyster bars, a bowling alley, a Masonic Lodge, a library, and four churches.[4] The heart of the port though was its commercial district, which was dominated by forty-three identical brick and granite warehouses. During the business season, which peaked between Christmas and May, pedestrians found the streets cluttered with the ubiquitous cotton bale and thronged with draymen, stevedores, cotton merchants, and sailors.

Generally, the boats that called on Apalachicola had all departed by 1 July of each year, not to return again until mid-December when the river was again high enough to transport the new season's cotton to market. By the end of the 1844 business season, sixty-two sea craft had entered Apalachicola Bay from New York alone. Other American boats had arrived from Mobile; St. Marks, Florida; Charleston; New Orleans; Boston; Key West; Baltimore; Providence, Rhode Island; Galveston; Portsmouth, Massachusetts; and Portland and Waldboro, Maine. Foreign vessels arriving in Apalachicola that season hailed from Havana and Matanzas, Cuba; Puerto Rico; Liverpool; Le Havre; St. Thomas, Virgin Islands; Turk Island, West Indies; Point Petre; Jamaica; and Marseilles.[5] The previous season had brought 398 boats into the harbor, and 244 vessels arrived in the 1844–45 season.[6]

These vessels often found their journey to Apalachicola a hazardous one. The passage from a domestic port such as New York to Apalachicola was actually riskier than making a transatlantic passage since danger lay, not in the open sea, but in the hazards near the shoreline.[7] Furthermore, the trip from a northern port to the Gulf was safer than the return trip. When sailing northward, the captain had only to follow the Gulf Stream while the southbound course required following a weaker shoreline current that brought boats dangerously close to the shoals off Cape Hatteras, North Carolina.[8]

The most dangerous area of all in reaching the Gulf of Mexico was in rounding the tip of Florida. There, in the Bahamas and the Florida Keys, seamen had to pick their way painstakingly among the dangerous reefs and islands that separated the Atlantic from the Gulf of Mexico, often against strong conflicting currents and without the aid of sufficient navigational markers.[9] Between the years 1844 and 1851, 279 vessels were wrecked in these waters,[10] which explains why the major industry of Key West was salvaging.[11]

The ship *Moro Castle* sailed through these waters early in 1860, and its surviving log describes a typical coastwise voyage. Had Captain W. L. Knowles believed in omens he might never have sailed for Apalachicola that February. As the towboat came alongside the ship in New York harbor, the captain found that both his mates were drunk and only four of his sailors were on board. For five hours he attempted to round up the rest of the crew. Meanwhile, a gale blew up. Because the towboat could not make headway against the storm, the ship was compelled to anchor until it subsided, and Knowles was unable to commence his voyage until the following day.[12]

Once underway, though, the ship averaged about 150 miles per day on its way south. By 4 March 1860, the ship was safely through "Hole in the Wall," the often perilous channel between the Abacos and the Eleutheras in the Bahama Islands, and was heading eastward

The Port of Apalachicola in 1837
(Florida State Archives)

toward the Berry Islands. The following day the captain sighted the lighthouse on Great Isaac Island, north of Bimini. The course among these islands and around the Florida Keys was so narrow that it created a bottleneck for traffic in and out of the Gulf of Mexico. The captain saw many vessels in these waters, some of which he knew on sight. Gentle breezes and the lighthouses at Sombrero Key, Key West, Sand Cay, and the Tortugas aided him in passing safely into the Gulf.[13]

The *Moro Castle* fortunately experienced good weather during the trickiest part of its passage. The captain traveled with his wife and daughter, a fairly common practice by 1860, and he noted that they were "quite well and able to do their duty at the table."[14] As the ship rounded Tortugas and turned northward toward Apalachicola, Knowles towed a fishing line astern and caught a Spanish mackerel. After a "fine supper" of fresh fish the captain wrote "the day ends very pleasantly. Wife ironing."[15]

By morning, though, the ship encountered a bitter north wind and heavy seas. The captain ordered the topgallant sails down. When the winds increased in velocity, he had the topsails double-reefed and the mainsail and outer jib taken in. An hour later the crew also close-reefed the topsails and took in the foresail jib. The captain's family became seasick, and even the seafarer admitted the seas were "quite rough." All was not unpleasant, however; he caught another fish.[16]

For the next three days the deckhands struggled to lower or reef the ship's many sails as the winds continued to howl, and the captain confided to his journal, "I have not a doubt but what we should have been safely at anchor in the harbor of Apalachicola ere this a few days ago. I did not dream of a gale here."[17] After fighting the storm for five days the captain finally sighted Dog Island light and with the aid of the harbor pilot soon was moored safely inside St. George Sound.[18]

After the business of entering the vessel had been attended to, the captain and his family went into town where they no doubt met Mrs. Henry Moulton, the wife of another seafarer, who kept a journal of her travels in the bark *Kepler*.[19] Once a vessel had anchored in the bay, captains and their families usually stayed in a hotel while the ship's crew spent weeks in unloading freight or ballast and reloading another cargo. During that time the wives socialized with one another. Mrs. Moulton enjoyed long walks with other women "out to the store and into the cotton press" and "beyond the wind mill some ways, and round by the beach back to Mr. Hancock's."[20]

She also visited every church in town, even the black church, which was popular among the white maritime visitors to Apalachicola because of its vibrant music. Almost daily she paid a social call to the wife of one of her husband's associates, and she recorded the comings and goings of other captains and their wives in her journal. "Mrs. Chandler expects to go down to their vessel today," she wrote on 6 March 1860. The next day she penned, "Mrs. Willis went back to their Ship." A week later she mentioned that "Capt. Curtis & wife went down to their vessel."[21]

While the captains and their families socialized in town, there was much activity back at the boat. The ship *Sarah Parker* sailed into Apalachicola Bay from Liverpool in 1838 with a load of salt. While the captain was ashore, the crew unloaded the cargo via several schooners to be lightered into town. The process of unloading twenty-five hundred sacks of salt was no simple task; averaging only two hundred units per day, it took almost a month to complete the job. Once the hold of the ship was cleared, the captain hired a stevedore from town to stow the new cargo of cotton, and another month was consumed.[22]

The sea craft that sailed into Apalachicola Bay were of five types, depending on their size, the number of their masts, and their rigging.[23] Sloops were the smallest of all the merchant vessels. They had a single mast that supported a fore-and-aft sail (the sails ran in a line parallel to the length of the vessel). Sloops skirted the coastline on their way between New York, Apalachicola, and Mobile, but also occasionally carried cotton and passengers between Apalachicola and St. Marks, the closest Florida port to the east.

Schooners had two or more masts that were also fore-and-aft rigged. They were the workhorses of the coasting trade because even though they had great storage capacity, the sail configuration only required a small crew,[24] and their relatively shallow draft allowed them to pass over the sandbars that blocked the bigger vessels from entry into most Gulf harbors. For these reasons they often were employed as lighters in loading and unloading the larger craft that were compelled to anchor some distance away from the city docks. The average schooner calling on Apalachicola in 1844 was 88 tons, but they ranged in size from the 49-ton *Cape Cod* to the 149-ton *Octavia*.[25] Between January and July 1844, eighty-six schooners docked at Apalachicola. About one-half (49 percent) ran between Apalachicola and New Orleans, and 18 percent came from Havana, Cuba. Of all schooners leaving Apalachicola 14 percent cleared for New York.[26]

Brigs, which were generally larger in tonnage than the schooners, had two masts but were square-rigged. (Their sails ran in a line perpendicular to the length of the boat.) Brigs calling on Apalachicola in 1844 averaged 211 tons burthen. Seventy percent of the Apalachicola brig trade ran between Apalachicola and New York.

Next largest in size came the bark, which had three masts with the forward two masts square-rigged and the third mast fore-and-aft rigged.[27] About one-half of the barks touching at Apalachicola during the season ending in 1844 came from and were destined to New York. The next most common destinations for barks clearing Apalachicola were Boston and Liverpool.[28]

The queen of the sailing fleet was the full-rigged ship, which had three masts, all of which bore square-rigging.[29] (Technically the term "ship" can only be applied to this last type of vessel. Schooners, barks, and brigs are not "ships.") As was the case with the barks, about one-half of the ships that touched at Apalachicola during the 1843–44 season were en route to or from New York. Only 12 percent of the ships leaving Apalachicola in 1844 cleared directly for Liverpool. Indeed, if all the larger craft (brigs, barks, and ships) that departed Apalachicola between January and July 1844 are combined, the dominance of the port of New York in Apalachicola's cotton trade is evident. Fifty-nine percent of the departures were to New York compared with only 11 percent which cleared directly for Liverpool.[30] Sixty percent of those larger vessels entering Apalachicola had also come from New York.

New York's dominance over Apalachicola's trade is curious since Apalachicola's exports were almost exclusively cotton, and New York had no textile industry. From New York, however, the cotton was transshipped to New England or to European mills. Why was it that Apalachicola cotton did not move directly to its destination?

New York was the first American port to establish transatlantic shipping on a regular basis. As early as 1818 the "Black Ball Line" sailed between New York and Liverpool, keeping to an advertised schedule that was a welcome innovation. The certainty of their arrival and departure dates made these line ships instantly popular, and their success inspired competitors to enter the lucrative trade as well.[31] Operators of these packet lines found their eastbound cargoes unprofitable because Europe did not need or want New York's local products. They soon came to depend on southern cotton to fill their vessels. Southerners also relied on New York as a financial center. Marine insurance and commercial financing, for instance, were arranged there more easily than in any other port. Southern cotton destined for the mills of Manchester or Massachusetts thus was detoured through New York by fleets of coasting vessels.

Reliance solely on shipping figures to determine where Apalachicola cotton was exported can be misleading. Though only 14 percent of the bigger vessels sailed directly to Europe in 1844, the volume of cotton destined there that year was much greater since the largest vessels with superior cargo capacity dominated the transatlantic trade. Tables 2-1 and 2-2 tabulate where Apalachicola cotton was exported in the years for which statistics are available. On average about 40 percent of Apalachicola cotton went directly to Europe in the 1840s and 1850s,[32] while New York receipts from the Florida port averaged 24 percent.

Because 60 percent of the larger boats that sailed into Apalachicola had either come from or were destined to New York and one-quarter of Apalachicola's cotton was shipped directly to New York, the bonds between these two ports were obviously strong. Oddly, it seems the neighboring Gulf port of Mobile did not share

**Table 2-1.** Apalachicola Foreign Exports*

| | Percentage of Total Bales of Cotton Exported | | | | |
| Year | Liverpool | Havre | Antwerp | Other | Total Europe |
| --- | --- | --- | --- | --- | --- |
| 1843 | | | | | 46 |
| 1845 | 31 | 2 | | 8 | 41 |
| 1846 | 35 | 5 | | 1 | 41 |
| 1847 | 27 | 2 | | 4 | 33 |
| 1848 | 34 | | | 6 | 40 |
| 1850 | 23 | | 7 | 2 | 32 |
| 1851 | 32 | 7 | 5 | 2 | 46 |
| 1852 | 28 | 1 | 6 | 6 | 41 |
| 1853 | 29 | 3 | 3 | 3 | 38 |
| 1857 | 35 | | 4 | | 39 |
| 1858 | 37 | | | | 37 |

*Percentages were tabulated based on a statistical year, August to July. See Apalachicola *Commercial Advertiser,* 8 January 1844, 21 July 1846, 6 October 1847, 22 July 1848, and 10 March 1858; *Commercial Advertiser Prices Current,* 14 April 1851, 9 May 1853.

this association with New York. An early scholar of the New York packet lines concluded that Mobile's cotton "did not travel to any extent by the way of New York."[33] Instead, during the 1850s Mobile sent between 35 and 50 percent of its cotton directly to New Orleans.[34]

Apalachicola and Mobile had remarked different trade patterns, given their proximity to each other. The two ports also had little intercourse between themselves, for cotton was the primary export of both. Mobile was a strong trading partner of New Orleans, but this was a unique relationship not duplicated by any other southern port.[35]

Apalachicola contributed very little to the Crescent City's receipts. New Orleans received less than 7 percent of all Apalachicola exports on average during the fifteen years prior to the Civil War. This paltry amount is even more remarkable considering the

Table 2-2.   Apalachicola Coastwise Exports*

Percentage of Total Bales of Cotton Exported

| Year | New York | Boston | Providence | New Orleans | Other | Total |
|------|----------|--------|------------|-------------|-------|-------|
| 1845 | 26 | 17 | 6 | 6 | 4 | 59 |
| 1846 | 32 | 12 | 7 | 2 | 6 | 59 |
| 1847 | 22 | 17 | 7 | 15 | 6 | 67 |
| 1848 | 32 | 19 | 5 | 2 | 2 | 60 |
| 1850 | 22 | 24 | 10 | 7 | 5 | 68 |
| 1851 | 24 | 16 | 4 | 8 | 2 | 54 |
| 1852 | 27 | 20 | 6 | 1 | 5 | 59 |
| 1853 | 16 | 35 | 6 | 2 | 3 | 62 |
| 1857 | 14 | 34 | 6 | 1 | 6 | 61 |
| 1858 | 25.5 | 9.5 | | 24 | 4 | 63 |

*Percentages were tabulated based on a statistical year, August to July. See Apalachicola *Commercial Advertiser,* 21 July 1846, 6 October 1847, 22 July 1848, and 10 March 1858; *Commercial Advertiser Prices Current,* 14 April 1851, 9 May 1853.

number of vessels that sailed between these two ports. During the 1844 commercial season, thirty-nine schooners (46 percent of all schooners entering Apalachicola that year) arrived from New Orleans and forty-two (or 49 percent) cleared Apalachicola for New Orleans.[36]

Because so many of these boats were engaged in the New Orleans to Apalachicola shuttle, and so little of Apalachicola's exports moved to New Orleans,[37] it appears the eastbound leg of this round trip was so lucrative that it compensated for meager returns on the westbound trip. In fact, the account books of one schooner captain who sailed regularly between Apalachicola and New Orleans during two different seasons demonstrate that at least one boat often lost money on the Florida to Louisiana run.[38]

Between January and June in 1851, Captain Robert Norris sailed the schooner *General Clinch* between the two ports eight times. On each trip he tallied both his expenses and his income on freight. By season's end, the vessel had made $2,170.62 on the four eastbound runs, but had *lost* a total of $145.88 on the voyages out of Apalachicola. The next year the deficits on the Apalachicola to New Orleans run were even greater; he lost $457.51 on the westbound leg of his journeys. In fact, on one voyage to New Orleans Norris could find no freight at all in Apalachicola, so he bought 150 bags of salt there for fifty cents each, transported them to New Orleans, and resold them for sixty-five cents. Even with the captain's enterprising efforts, the profit on the trip after lighterage and commissions were deducted amounted to only $7.57.[39]

As far as exports from Apalachicola are concerned, the port of Boston, Massachusetts, was a more significant trade partner than New Orleans. Boston received an average of 20 percent of all cotton exported from Apalachicola in those years for which data exist.[40] Francis Cabot Lowell, the Massachusetts textile pioneer, bought a large portion of the raw cotton he needed for his world-renowned factory from Apalachicola agents.[41] A good deal of cotton moved northward from Apalachicola in the holds of Boston-based vessels. Ten percent of the larger vessels clearing Apalachicola in 1844 ran to the New England port. According to Samuel Eliot Morison, New Englanders also had an interest in cotton bound for New York, either by virtue of owning the cotton or the vessels.[42]

The port of Providence, Rhode Island, also received a substantial proportion of Apalachicola cotton. During seven of the ten years for which export figures exist, this port received more Apalachicola cotton than New Orleans did.

Apalachicola truly was a cotton port. It exported little else other than a few items used to fill vessels when enough cotton was unavailable. During the peak of the 1843–44 shipping season, when cotton exports totaled 105,934 bales,[43] there was little other freight going out of Apalachicola. For example, other than the approximately 54,000 bales of cotton exported to New York in those months, vessels clearing Apalachicola for the northern port carried 29 boxes of tobacco, several barrels of beeswax, one box of tallow, 10 tons of iron, 4,806 "sticks" of cedar plus 4,114 feet of cedar, 62 mahogany logs, and 31 cords of firewood. Of these exports the iron and mahogany were, no doubt, being transshipped from another port as the river's hinterland did not produce them.

Coasting schooners that year transported 150 sacks of cotton seed, 16 bales of cotton fabric, 3 bales of gunny bags, 238 sacks of coffee, and 25 cords of firewood to New Orleans. Ships bound for Liverpool carried 154 "sticks" of cedar. Vessels sailing to Boston hauled four thousand pipe staves in addition to the usual cargo of cotton. Firewood and a few head of cattle went to Key West, and Havana received 525 empty barrels, 31 empty casks, and 5,000 staves.[44] All the remaining cargo leaving Apalachicola that season was cotton.

Apalachicola was an important cotton export center, but it was insignificant as a port of entry. For example, the cotton that was exported from there during the 1842–43 season had a value of $3,068,500, while the value of imports in that year totaled only $44,771.[45] The exported cotton was worth about sixty-nine times the value of Apalachicola's incoming freight.

Historians of the antebellum economy continue to debate the degree of self-sufficiency attained on southern farms and plantations and the dimensions of the trade in foodstuffs and provisions flowing from the West[46] to the Cotton South. Some authorities, such as Louis Schmidt and Douglass North, held that southern plantations were so specialized in the production of cotton that the planters were compelled to import most of their food, and thus they served as an important impetus to the development of the West.[47] Other scholars have concluded that the rural South was largely self-sufficient and its imports of food really were negligible.[48]

While it can be seen from Table 2-3 that Apalachicola imported quite a lot of "western" products, the river valley was virtually self-sufficient. For example, during the 1844 shipping season when the entire river valley received its supplies via Apalachicola, 117,488 pounds of corn were imported from New Orleans. This sum seems rather large until one considers the size of the population of the river valley in that year, which topped 146,000.[49] If the importation figures are accurate, the per capita importation of corn in 1844 amounted to only .8 pounds. Even if the data published in the local

**Table 2-3.**   Apalachicola Imports, 1 January 1844–30 June 1844*

## Imports from New Orleans

498 barrels (15,687 gallons) of molasses
990 sacks (198,000 lbs.) of coffee
911 sacks (195,865 lbs.) of salt
281 hogsheads and 164 barrels of sugar
250 bushels and 616 sacks (117,488 lbs.) of corn
1,011 barrels (31,846.5 gallons) of whiskey
1,394 barrels (273,224 lbs.) of flour
223 kegs (22,300 lbs.) of lard
214 casks and 14 hogsheads of bacon
158 barrels (31,600 lbs.) of pork
10 barrels (2,000 lbs.) of beef
14,072 packages of "merchandise"
12 bales and 1,372 pieces of bagging
1308 coils of rope
212 barrels (approx. 42,400 lbs.) of potatoes
13 casks of cheese
2.5 barrels (500 lbs.) of mackerel
4.5 barrels of cranberries
6 boxes and 1 hogshead of tobacco
1 cotton press screw
1 anchor
16 reels of packing yarn
8 stoves
10 kettles
2 crates
36 plough molds
10 kegs of white lead

**Table 2-3.** continued

---

### Imports from New York

25,041 packages of "merchandise"
3 tons of white lead
430 bales of hay
250 tons of ice
200 sacks (43,000 lbs.) of salt
23,000 bricks

### Imports from Havana

1,167 sacks (233,400 lbs.) of coffee
1,435 barrels, 507 tierces, and 50 hogsheads
    (69,646.5 gals.) of molasses
237,000 and 22 boxes of cigars
8 boxes, 1 barrel, and 43 hogsheads of sugar
25 cases of sweetmeats
5 casks of cheese
"Fruit" (amount unspecified)
Merchandise (uncounted)

### Imports from Mobile

10,619 sacks (1,141.54 tons) of salt
314 packages of "merchandise"

### Imports from Charleston

18,000 feet of lumber
72 hogsheads of coal
25 casks of rice
1,059 packages, 2 casks, and 1 barrel of "merchandise"
100 barrels (approx. 10 tons) of potatoes
100 casks of lime

continued

**Table 2-3.** continued

### Imports from Providence

300 barrels (approx. 30 tons) of potatoes
150 casks of lime

### Imports from Liverpool

7,600 sacks (817 tons) of salt
30 barrels (approx. 3 tons) of potatoes
8 casks of porter

### Imports from Baltimore

Unspecified amounts of "Merchandise" and "Castings"

### Imports from Boston

300 bars of iron
800 casks of lime
5 casks of plaster
27 kegs of nails
521 packages of "merchandise"
400 empty barrels

### Imports from Turks Island

2,984 bushels (119.36 tons) of salt
3 tons of Brazil wood
Unspecified amounts of "fruit"

### Imports from St. Marks

214 bales of cotton

*These statistics were compiled using ships' manifests recorded weekly in the Apalachicola *Commercial Advertiser*. Calculations were made using the following equivalents: a barrel equals 31.5 gallons, 1 tierce equals 42 gallons, 1 hogshead equals 63 gallons, 1 sack equals 3 bushels, 1 bushel of corn equals 56 lbs., 1 barrel of flour equals 196 lbs., 1 keg equals 100 lbs.

newspaper were incomplete or inaccurate, one could arrive at the same conclusion by quadrupling the estimate of corn importation. The same was true for the importation of meat into the river valley. During the 1844 season, the per capita importation of pork and beef collectively amounted to less than a quarter of a pound.[50]

More than any other commodity, salt was the cargo of incoming vessels. From January through June 1844, 2,197.3 tons of salt were landed at the Apalachicola wharf (about half of which came from Mobile). Salt and other bulky commodities like hay, potatoes,[51] and lime were essentially used as ballast by the vessels destined for Apalachicola and other southern ports. Ship captains would rather carry these commodities at cheap rates than to have to procure other ballast that paid them nothing.[52]

Depending on the itineraries they kept and their punctuality, the vessels that called on Apalachicola could be categorized as either "transients," "regular traders," or "packets." The "transient" boats moved from port to port at the whim of their captains. They picked up a cargo wherever they could find one and carried it to whatever port was required. Often they corresponded with each other in care of their home ports, and two surviving letters written from Apalachicola describe the spontaneity required of the transient vessels. Captain Edward B. Jenkins wrote a fellow seaman in 1840, saying, "I had the opportunity of loading for this place soon after you left and took in Eleven hundred barrels. . . . had a fine passage of two days only from N. O."[53] Captain Edmond B. Mallet wrote a letter from Apalachicola to the same man reporting on his and others' whereabouts in 1852: "I am all ready for Sea bound to Boston with a Six thousand dollar freight in the Ship—rather better than I could of don [*sic*] in New Orleans. . . . tell [Captain Strickland] that Old Crowell is hear [*sic*] landing for Boston tell Capt. S. I arrived here the Same day Crowell did thirty one days from Havre."[54]

The life of a transient sailor might seem exciting, but life at sea was anything but idyllic. Black sailors were arrested and jailed for the duration of their ship's stay in Apalachicola.[55] Even white crewmen were treated little better than slaves. Captain Edward Marshall wrote from Apalachicola in 1843 that he had picked up three crewmen in Boston who had caused him nothing but trouble. The trio refused to work, whereupon Marshall went to town and had them jailed. Upon his return to the boat, the captain discovered that two other crew members had been "stolen out of the Ship by some Boat from Town."[56]

Contrasting with the transient vessels were the "regular traders," which generally sailed between two or more specific ports. Robert Norris's movements aboard the schooner *General Clinch* during the 1851 season are characteristic of a regular trader. Norris began and ended the cotton season in New York, but during the shipping season he made eight passages between New Orleans and Apalachicola.[57] Once the cotton season had ended, Norris and the other captains who regularly made Apalachicola calls found there was no freight to be had there. For that reason these vessels found work elsewhere during the summer until it was time to return to the South for the cotton season. During the 1844 season, the schooners *Lion, Seminole, Swallow,* and *Textor* all ran between New Orleans and Apalachicola but cleared for New York at season's end.[58]

Packet liners were the third category of vessel that served Apalachicola. Packets could be of any type of boat from sloop to ship so long as they ran on an advertised schedule. The smallest packet boat to serve Apalachicola was the sloop *Ellen* that left weekly for St. Marks in 1840. It carried up to six passengers and twenty barrels.[59] There were also packet schooners, like the *Octavia* that ran between New Orleans and Apalachicola in 1844.[60] Sailing ships and steam-propelled sternwheelers also advertised they would make regular trips between two points. One steam propeller boat ran between New Orleans and Apalachicola in 1844.[61]

Packet service between these two ports continued throughout the 1850s. The steamship *America* made regular trips "during the season" beginning in 1852.[62] Ship operations were suspended in January 1854, "in consequence of the high price of coal," but the company promised to resume trade again when the price of fuel had declined "to a living price."[63] The ship was back in service in the fall, advertising it would leave New Orleans "about every ten days."[64] The *America* continued its service to New Orleans for at least four more years.[65]

In addition to this line the Southern Steamship Company called bimonthly at Apalachicola during the 1857 and 1858 seasons. The Southern line ships *Atlantic* and *Calhoun* sailed from New Orleans calling each day at another port beginning with Pensacola, then Apalachicola, St. Marks, Cedar Keys, and Tampa, before reaching Key West and reversing the order.[66] Another packet line to run between New Orleans and Apalachicola applied for a Florida charter in 1858.[67]

Apalachicola also had a bimonthly packet service to Charleston during two business seasons,[68] but New York packet lines were the most numerous of all. Elisha Hurlbut, a New Yorker, originated the first New York/Apalachicola packet line in 1825. Service was irregular during the first five years of its existence, but in 1830 Hurlbut set a bimonthly schedule for the line.[69] By 1843 the Hurlbut line employed three ships and three brigs and promised to "sail punctually as advertised" during the season.[70] The following season, Hurlbut added a fourth ship to the line, but two of the vessels never actually called at Apalachicola in that year.[71]

Those vessels of the Hurlbut line that did come into Apalachicola during that year shuttled between New York and Apalachicola, and did not follow the "cotton triangle" attributed to Hurlbut's New York/Mobile packet line.[72] Robert Albion concluded that since Mobile had only cotton to offer as outgoing freight, the vessels could find no cargo during the summer months before the new crop of cotton was harvested. Therefore, it came to be Hurlbut's practice to send his vessels from Mobile to Liverpool at the end of the season. The ship transported general freight and passengers from Europe to New York, then sailed southward during the cotton marketing season for another cargo of cotton. According to Albion, the Mobile packets eventually began to sail the "triangle" twice a year, and direct trips from Mobile to New York became scarce by 1850.[73]

During the same time period, Hurlbut's Apalachicola liners did not follow this shipping pattern, even though it also had nothing to offer as outgoing freight at the end of the cotton season. None of Hurlbut's Apalachicola liners cleared for Europe in 1844.[74]

The rival packet service known as the Star Line also served as a

New York to Apalachicola shuttle service in 1844 without making the "triangle." This line advertised that it would use two ships and six brigs,[75] but like the Hurlbut line, two of the vessels never entered Apalachicola Bay. The vessels of both lines made either one or two round trips between the American ports during January and July 1844, and most were back in operation as the new season began in the fall of that year.

Most of the vessels calling at Apalachicola in that year were not packets, but they did not generally follow the "triangle" either. Of the 14 percent of all the larger vessels leaving Apalachicola and sailing directly for Europe in that year,[76] only one-half of those on which complete information exists made the classic triangular voyage by arriving from a northern American port and clearing Apalachicola for Europe.[77] Instead of moving around the triangle, most of the large vessels that called on Apalachicola in 1844 came from and were destined to New York.

The remuneration these vessels received for transporting Apalachicola's cotton fluctuated. Like cotton prices, freight rates were dependent on a number of variables, but the phenomenon of supply and demand was most important. An explanation of how their correlation could nudge up the price was given in the *Commercial Advertiser* in 1844: "The full stock of cotton for shipment and limited number of vessels have caused an advance of 1/52c [per pound] in an engagement for Boston; and on two for New York 1/16c advance. Masters now steadily refuse to take less than 9/16c for New York and 5/8c for Boston."[78]

The nature of the cargo also had some bearing on the price of transportation. If the cotton was packed in large round bales which took up more room than the more compressed square bales, the freight was naturally higher. The total amount of cotton a merchant shipped also affected the price of freight. Carriers gladly gave quantity discounts because the fewer the consignees needed to fill the hold, the better.[79]

In the course of a business season, prices often fluctuated widely. For example, during the 1844 season freight charges from Apalachicola to New York bounced around from $1 to $4 per bale. Rates

Steamer *Shamrock*, believed to be at Apalachicola wharf circa 1860s
(Florida State Archives)

to Liverpool that year bottomed at $3.75 and peaked at $7.50 per bale.[80]

Marine insurance rates were less volatile than freight rates, for they reflected the hazards of the sea more than any other factor. Ocean travel was a risky business. If seamen did not fall prey to the perils of rounding the tip of Florida, they might wreck while entering East Pass, as the ship *Henry* did in 1846, or even while in the comparative safety of St. George Sound, as the bark *Kepler* did in 1860.[81]

Besides the worry of running into the Florida coastline, there was also hurricane season to contend with just as the cotton season got underway each autumn. Without modern communication devices, mariners were especially vulnerable to violent weather. Scores of vessels were destroyed at Key West during the hurricanes of 1844 and 1846.[82] Similarly, the steamer *Lamplighter*, caught in a gale just outside of East Pass in 1841, drifted out to sea leaving no trace.[83]

Fires were another peril that insurers had to consider inasmuch as

cotton was a highly flammable cargo. Errant embers from the stevedores' pipes caused many fires while the boat was being loaded,
and when at sea the sun rays' concentration through the deck lights
often sparked the vessel's ruin.[84] From January 1859 to May 1860,
two barks and a ship burned while at anchor in Apalachicola Bay, and
a fourth vessel, sailing from Apalachicola to Norwich, also burned.[85]

Given these hazards, cotton shippers would have been foolhardy
not to insure their cargo. The added expense of 1¼ to 2 percent for
voyages between the Gulf of Mexico and New York or 1¼ to 2¾ to
and from Europe was well worth it.[86] Indeed, when the price of
cotton in New York or Europe fell below a profitable resale level,
the Apalachicola merchant undoubtedly prayed for the destruction
of his insured cargo en route.

The saltwater craft that called on antebellum Apalachicola,
whether diminutive sloops or tall ships, whether packets that sailed
on schedule or transients that followed only fortune, all relied on
cotton as their mainstay. They arrived in Florida's premier cotton
port at the opening of every commercial season, and they returned
there as long as they could expect to make a cargo.

So long as they continued to call there, Apalachicola's cotton
factors marked time by their arrival, for news came under sail. Boats
brought newspapers from other markets and letters from associates.
Passengers from other ports arrived with intelligence from the outside world, which was disseminated and dissected over drinks in
local taverns. Every crumb of information was devoured by these
communication-starved entrepreneurs whose best advantage lay in
having more information than their competitors.

The longer the period between arrivals, the more nervous and
tentative factors became in their decisions until business was suspended altogether on the eve of an expected landfall. Whenever a
new set of sails was spotted entering the bay, the townspeople
prickled with anticipation, and captains were undoubtedly greeted
at the dock by a bevy of businessmen eager to buy a sailor a drink
and listen to the latest from Liverpool. In a cotton port such as Apalachicola, land-loving merchants and salty seafarers had much to
talk about.

# 3

## *Cotton Money*

$\mathcal{T}$HE APALACHICOLA/CHATTAHOOCHEE RIVER VALLEY, ISO-
lated from other regions by the pine forests that enclosed it
and bound to the river that represented its primary commercial
artery, developed as a separate economy based on cotton with a distinctive circulating medium. This local currency consisted of a variegated
assortment of mostly paper bills supplemented by a few foreign and
native coins. An examination of the monetary conditions of this particular economy is necessary to our understanding of what business
conditions of the antebellum period were truly like. Every successful
businessman had to understand currency conditions and manipulate
them to his advantage. This dimension of commerce in antebellum
America has often been neglected, but in order to comprehend fully the
challenges each entrepreneur faced, we must begin with his currency.

Each river economy of the antebellum period developed at differ-
ing rates. Larry Schweikart has categorized the southern states
according to their economic history as being either part of the "Old
South" or of the "New South," labels that have no relationship to
their traditional meanings. According to Schweikart, the Old South
states of Virginia, the Carolinas, Georgia, and Louisiana, had a
longer history of commercial activity that enabled them to develop
banking regulations that tended to foster commercial growth.

Schweikart described the New South as being composed of the states of Alabama, Florida, Arkansas, Mississippi, and Tennessee, where "vigorous commercial histories" were lacking, and the state governments meddled in commercial policy to their own detriment.[1]

Situated between the political boundaries of Schweikart's Old and New South was the cotton economy of the Apalachicola/Chattahoochee River valley, which encompasses the "New South" states of Alabama and Florida, as well as the "Old South" state of Georgia. Banking policy and regulation within the valley differed from state to state, and these uneven conditions profoundly affected the character of the currency conditions within the valley. Even though they mirrored in many ways the economic environment of other developing economies, this particular set of circumstances gave this valley's monetary conditions its peculiar character.

Economically speaking, the antebellum era was one of wild mood swings. The booming 1830s that were fueled by cheap land prices (relative to other prices) and rising cotton profits were followed abruptly by a major depression in 1837.[2] That year cotton prices fell precipitously and, despite a short recovery in 1838, continued downward through 1842. Money that had formerly flowed into the South to pay for cotton no longer compensated for southern debts in the North. The South's cotton merchants and growers found themselves ensnared by a depreciating currency with which to repay their increasing indebtedness.

Those businessmen who weathered this great depression faced a new set of conditions in the last fifteen years of the antebellum period. The late 1840s and 1850s were again a time of phenomenal growth in which cotton prices rebounded and continued to rise. Only the brief Panic of 1857 disturbed the valley's prosperity in the years just prior to the Civil War.

Juxtaposed against this wildly fluctuating national economy was an equally volatile media of exchange. In the absence of a uniform currency provided by the federal government, every local economy had a distinctive currency that originated from scores of businessmen who held disparate assets—and consciences.

The coins in use in the United States in the antebellum period were a motley lot. They were not uniform in appearance because the government permitted private agencies, as well as its own mints, to coin gold. But American coins were only a small part of the specie in circulation in this country. In fact, they were not even the predominant coins. Since the sixteenth century the primary coin in America was the Spanish peso, also known as the piece-of-eight, but in America it was most commonly called the Spanish dollar. From the Spanish mints in Mexico and Peru it primarily found its way into the South via the West Indies.[3]

The Spanish dollar consisted of eight reales. Its fractional coins were the four-real piece (equal to the half-dollar), the double real (worth a quarter-dollar), the real (worth twelve and one-half cents), the half real or medio, and the quarter real.[4] Mingled with the Spanish and American coins were English sterling pounds that each comprised twenty shillings of twelve pence. These coins were intermixed so that in everyday business transactions Americans had to calculate in three currencies: one decimal; another based on halves, quarters, and eighths; and the third on twelfths and twentieths.

The amalgamation of these different coins and their appellations produced its own idiom. The Spanish real was convertible into the English shilling or "six-penny bit," which was over time shortened to a "bit." Southerners called both the Spanish and the English coin by this same name, and the U.S. quarter-dollar was "two bits."[5] The inaccurate term "penny" used for "cent" is also an anachronism that survived this period.[6]

The Spanish real's closest equivalent in English sterling was eleven pence. Many Americans eventually contracted "eleven pence" to "levy" so that a Spanish real was alternately called a "levy." Both the Spanish medio and the American half-dime, each roughly equivalent to "five pence," were known as a "fip."[7] In Columbus, Georgia, the Spanish half-real was called a "thrip,"[8] almost certainly because it was closest in value to an English "three-pence."

To complicate matters further, the combination of the coins of these different nationalities produced even more jargon. For instance, residents of Columbus called the combination of a "thrip" and seven pence a "ten-penceapenny." The American quarter-dollar united with seven pence was called a "one-a-ninepence."[9]

Although "Spanish" coins were predominant, many other foreign coins circulated as legal tender in the United States in the antebellum period, especially those of France, Scandinavia, and the German states. In 1847 the *Merchants' Magazine* published a table showing the current value in U.S. money of the gold and silver coins "in most general circulation" in the country. Of the one hundred varieties of gold and silver coins from thirty-six different countries listed, only nine were native.[10] Merchants necessarily kept tables such as this one near at hand to ease their constant tasks of conversion.

More debilitating than the variety of specie was the shortage of it. According to one estimate, this nation's total circulation in 1830 of all coins below the value of a half-dollar was a crippling twenty-five cents per capita.[11] Columbus, Georgia, shared in this national problem, where a warning about counterfeit coins was supplemented by the comment, "The scarcity of money in this region renders us comparatively secure against this spurious currency, but still some old miser who now and then gathers a silver dollar may be imposed upon."[12]

During the financial disturbances following 1837 and 1857 when banks withheld all coins, conditions were even worse, and there was an actue shortage of all kinds of coins.[13] Any businessman who required small change was compelled to buy what coins he could find from a broker at a premium.[14]

Given the state of the nation's currency, businessmen were forced to take matters into their own hands. Individuals, municipalities, businesses, and banks issued "change bills" in the amounts of one dollar and less. Denominations commonly ran as small as six and one-quarter cents (which corresponded to the Spanish medio). These printed slips usually promised to pay the bearer the equivalent of the face value in specie (coins) or bank notes when they were presented to the originator. The many forms of change bills (all worth a dollar or less) were known by the pejorative term, "shinplasters," which is purported to have originated during the American Revolutionary War when a soldier used the worthless Continental currency to bandage his wounded leg.[15]

Merchants or bankers offered them as change to their customers who tendered them to other storekeepers in payment of their debts. The latter had little choice but to accept them and pass them along as change to their customers.[16] Therefore, by trading his pieces of paper for something of actual value the man who initiated the change bill had the use of another's money free of charge. Furthermore, the originator would never have to repay a certain percentage of this amount because few people bothered to redeem a bill for six and a quarter cents or the like, and many were lost or destroyed in the process of circulating.

During the financial spasm following the Panic of 1837, the valley of the Chattahoochee/Apalachicola River was awash in these slips of paper that were only as good as the man who issued them, and each entrepreneur had to judge for himself the worth of each one. John D. Howell, a drygoods merchant and part-time cotton dealer in Columbus, advertised that he would "receive in payment for his Goods all Change-Bills that he consider[ed] to be good."[17] A year later he announced that he would redeem his own change bills in "Specie or Specie Funds."[18] By 1843 the shortage of change had lessened and Howell announced he wished "to retire his Change Bills from circulation—there being now a sufficient amount of specie to answer the purposes of trade."[19]

H. T. Hall, who ran a cotton warehouse and commission business in Columbus, innovated the use of his personal checks on the Bank of Columbus as a change bill during one period when currency was scarce. After the monetary crisis had passed, he advertised locally that he would redeem them in "specie or its equivalent" on demand.[20] "Its equivalent" amounted to the notes of local banks that were solvent enough to be able to redeem their own notes in specie.

By the end of 1842, the shortage of change in Columbus was lessening. The cotton warehouse of Smith and Hayward advertised that they would redeem their change bills "if presented at their counting room."[21] The same edition of the local paper carried the advertisement of another cotton firm, Greenwood and Grimes, who announced that they were now redeeming their change bills in the notes of specie-paying banks.[22] The firm of Ruse and Barnard advertised that small specie change could be had there.[23] But private change bills were still in circulation in 1843,[24] and in 1848 the Columbus Grand Jury complained about the nuisance of so many of them.[25]

Many states were concerned about the prevalence of these promises to pay, which were much abused. They could be easily counterfeited, and their value was questionable because their collateral was unregulated and often nonexistent.[26] The possibilities for creating capital in this way did not escape a shrewd businessman, and the temptation was strong to circulate more of them than one could repay. A Columbus newspaper lamented this fact, saying: "There are persons in this town issuing their printed change bills & undertaking to furnish the people with a currency, whose banking capital if it exists at all is extremely apocryphal."[27]

Following the specious logic that to forbid change bills would force coins back into circulation all three states bordering the river valley outlawed them in some fashion. But there was a genuine need for them, and the persistent found loopholes. A common way to skirt the law of one state was to issue change bills for local use that purported to be from another state. This is probably why two manufacturing companies in Columbus issued twenty-five-cent scrips with "Apalachicola, Fla." printed on them.[28]

Alabama proclaimed that all such notes under one dollar in value must bear interest at the rate of "100 per cent per annum from date of issue."[29] "[B]ut necessity often makes man do the unlawful almost as readily as conscience makes him do his duty."[30] The law was a dead letter.

The territory of Florida prohibited the issue of notes of less than one dollar as early as 1828. When it became a state in 1845, its constitution forbade the release of notes under the value of five dollars.[31] Both these laws were generally ignored throughout the antebellum period in Apalachicola, Florida's largest commercial center.

Georgia passed a law similar to Florida's, but, as seen above, this statute did not stop the businessmen of Columbus. The worst offender was John G. Winter, the most prominent capitalist in Columbus. He circulated fifty thousand dollars worth in denominations of one dollar, twenty-five cents, and fifty cents.[32] To avoid prosecution these were ostensibly issued from Apalachicola. To avoid their redemption they were made payable in Charleston, South Carolina, or New York. Winter's personal change bills bore his portrait and the name of the bank he owned, which gave them the appearance of being official bank notes.[33] Not everyone was fooled. His most ardent critic said of them: "They are nothing more than bits of paper resting upon Mr. Winter's personal credit, and what is more uncertain Mr. Winter's life."[34]

Winter responded to this attack on their validity by publishing this notice: "Although they are not made payable here, for the convenience of the public they will be redeemed here. As persons have made it their business (for want of something better to do) to annoy the Teller by presenting one bill at a time, . . . the Teller will hereafter require that they shall be presented in sums of five dollars, and upwards."[35]

Beneath this notice the editor retorted: "Mr. Winter replies, 'they are good, and I will redeem them *here* (how amiable!) provided my Teller is not *annoyed* by their presentment too often, & in sums, too small!' . . . It is no trouble for the Teller to *issue* them, but it is an Intolerable bore to redeem them."[36]

The Georgia law that outlawed change bills provided that issuers of change bills were subject to a fine equal to five hundred dollars for each bill in circulation.[37] Because informers were eligible to receive one-half of the fine, the Columbus cotton merchant who reported the illegal activity to authorities was awarded $47,500 by the Muscogee County Superior Court.[38] Winter hired a sly lawyer to take care of the liability. Attorney Raphael Moses's defense centered on a case involving the Fugitive Slave Law in which the U.S. Supreme Court decided that an informer was not entitled to the reward until after judgment was rendered. According to this decision, if the statute was repealed before the judgment was made, the informers forfeited their rights to the reward.

If Moses could get the change bill law repealed he could use the

Fugitive Slave precedent to get his client off, so he drafted a new statute that repealed the fine but was more stringent respecting other aspects of banking than the original act.[39] Moses gave the draft to Winter who, with his connections, had no trouble in getting it through the legislature. The general public was completely taken in by the new law, believing it to be reform legislation.[40] Moses eventually appealed the case to the Supreme Court using the Fugitive Slave case as a precedent, and his client won.[41] Ironically, while Winter was circulating his own "shinplasters," his bank refused to accept the change bills of any other individual.[42] However, "Winter Change Bills" were still circulating in Columbus as late as 1857.[43]

Because of such smelly dealings the city of Columbus felt obliged to issue its own notes to "supersede those issued by private individuals."[44] Columbus businessmen much preferred the city change bills to private issues. In 1841, eighty-eight businessmen signed a petition vowing not to receive or pay out any other bills than those of the city of Columbus.[45]

Of course, the fact was not lost on city councilmen that many municipalities raised money in this way. Even though Columbus may have initiated the change bills as a public service, it appears the city later overextended itself in this fashion. Throughout the years 1843 to 1845, its scrip was traded in Columbus at a discount of from 10 to 20 percent when some private bills were worth their full value.[46] Nevertheless, people all over the valley used Columbus scrip. Denominations of twelve and one-half cents, twenty-five cents, fifty cents, and one dollar circulated in Apalachicola even though the latter city issued its own bills during the depression.[47]

Change bills represented only a portion of the nation's currency, and cotton merchants more frequently required larger denominations of money. Inasmuch as the federal government did not print any paper currency, most of the country's larger bills were issued by state banks.

Because the river passed through three different states, each with its own set of banking regulations, an examination of the valley's banking conditions is complicated threefold. The younger states of Alabama and Florida had similar banking histories. In both cases, the early experiences with state banks prior to the 1837 depression were so unsuccessful that both state legislatures virtually banned native banks. During most of the period between the depression and the Civil War, the businessmen of Apalachicola, as well as the entrepreneurs on the Alabama side of the river, used Georgia bank notes.

Bank notes generally commanded more respect from the populace than change bills because they were backed by the tangible (albeit often inadequate) stocks of coins held in reserve in the bank's vault. It has been estimated that between 1790 and 1865 sixteen hundred banks in thirty-four states issued over thirty thousand varieties of bank notes.[48] All these notes were different in appearance from any other. The assortment of bank notes in circulation with "no standardization of size or design"[49] boggles the mind of a modern student. There is no present need for advertisements such as the one seen in a Columbus newspaper in 1851 that announced a twenty-dollar bill found in a certain location. The owner could claim it by describing it.[50] William Graham Sumner described well their heterogeneity: "The bank notes were bits of paper recognizable as a specie by shape, color, size and engraved work. Any piece of paper which had these came within the prestige of money; the only thing in the shape of money to which the people were accustomed."[51]

The various bank notes circulating in the Chattahoochee/Apalachicola River region certainly fit this description. Although they were more uniform in size than change bills, their likeness ended there. Each bank designed its own notes that were embellished with engravings of gods and goddesses, sailing ships and steamboats.[52]

With so many different kinds of bills revolving in the valley, many crudely engraved, it was especially easy to alter or forge the genuine ones. Newspapers in both Columbus and Albany warned their readers of a gang of men in Columbus who were passing the counterfeited notes of two South Carolina banks.[53] These notes had been printed by the thieves and bore little resemblance to the genuine note.

There were other means of deception. Often the notes of a failed bank were stolen, its name obliterated and the name of a reputable bank printed in its place. The counterfeiters rarely noticed the symbolism of the remaining vignettes engraved on it. In this way the supposed note of a bank in Massachusetts came to have engravings of a cotton plant, Andrew Jackson, and the Georgia state coat of arms. The Southern Bank of Bainbridge, Georgia, had originally printed the note.[54]

The bank notes of John Winter's Bank of St. Mary's also fell victim to fraud. One rogue took a genuine five-dollar bill that had its value engraved across each end of the bill and altered it. He pasted over the "five" with the word "twenty" cut from a twenty-dollar bill of a broken Florida bank.[55] This method produced a common type of counterfeit known as a "raised note."[56]

Before taking the bill of an unfamiliar bank, the merchant scrutinized it for authenticity. He held it up to the light to look for the holes made by the thin pins on which bankers used to file their notes. If there were many holes it might indicate that they had been in circulation for some time and were probably good. Next he consulted his "bank note reporter and counterfeit detector," which listed hundreds of bank notes, the rate of discount of "uncurrent" notes (those trading below par), and a description of the known counterfeit notes of each bank.[57] Of course even these manuals could not be trusted when it came to the worth of a bank note because some were notorious for disinformation.[58] If the merchant was still unsure, he might either refuse it or accept it at a discount with the intention of passing it off on one of his customers as change.

Every banker understood that the longer he could keep his notes in circulation without being redeemed in specie the more credit he had created for his business at no interest. Therefore bankers devised ways of evading redemption.[59] The obvious method was to put one's notes in circulation as far away from his place of business as possible. Bankers often employed an agent known as a "carpetbagger" to initiate this circulation for them.[60] "[N]early every specie basis bank had its carpetbagger—a fellow it sent with notes by the carpet-bag full into some distant State to get them into circulation there."[61] The carpetbagger arranged with the banker of a distant town to swap notes. Because each set was redeemable only at the place of issue hundreds of miles away, it was improbable that persons who acquired the bills would ever go to the trouble of claiming their specie. For this reason it was said, "Illinois was flooded with Georgia notes."[62]

To compound profits, after a banker had given out all of another's notes he could refuse to receive them from customers, who were told to go to the local broker or "money shaver" to sell them. The latter would buy them only at a discount. Then, it was commonly believed, the broker and the banker would divide the profit.[63]

Few bankers were so unscrupulous, but even the most reputable ones scattered their notes as far away from them as they could. An agent for the cotton commission business of J. Day and Company of Apalachicola wrote from Georgia that he was leaving one thousand dollars with a colleague there because he had "promised to give the Bank bills circulations & he [the associate] can change them off."[64]

A banker who did not have the capital readily on hand to redeem his notes might also issue "post notes," which resembled standard bank notes except the bank promised to redeem them at some future date, ranging from three to twelve months. The Commercial Bank of Florida in Apalachicola floated these in denominations of five and ten dollars.[65]

The antebellum businessman was necessarily a student of the currency. Every bank note "circulated at a discount equal at least to the cost of bringing it back to the place of issue for redemption in hard money."[66] Notes of a bank known to be overextended were worth considerably less than this minimum rate. Any person whose business involved the acceptance of bank notes carefully monitored the going rates of the currency by reading the bank note tables published weekly in Columbus and Apalachicola.

All classes of the economy were hurt when a bank's notes were devalued. Merchants were injured because their expenses and risks were increased. The planter, as debtor at the bottom of the credit chain, bore the ultimate loss because it took more money to repay a debt than he originally had borrowed. When specie redemption was suspended by the local banks in times of financial crisis such as in 1837 and 1857, both the Florida merchants and their upriver customers suffered greatly as the value of their money dropped relative to those banks that were paying specie.

In 1841 the Apalachicola commission merchants were losing so much money by the rapid deflation of their currency they became desperate. "We have seen the notes of the Columbus Banks, which form our entire currency depreciate 15 or 20 per cent in less than sixty days. It is obvious that the merchant . . . cannot long continue business under such a system without ruin; the nature of every contract is changed and his whole property and business at the mercy of bankrupt and irresponsible corporations."[67]

The Floridians formally resolved to make all transactions on a specie basis (that is, to accept depreciated notes at their specie value only). They urged the other merchants and planters upriver to do likewise. Columbus merchants made the same vow the following year,[68] but there is no record of whether either group was successful.

Because the discounts on bank notes varied with the distance from the issuing bank, values changed as one moved down the long river valley. In Apalachicola in August 1843, notes of Georgia's Centrail Rail Road and Banking Company were trading at a 20 percent discount, those of the Central Bank of Georgia for 35 percent off, and the notes of the state bank of Alabama were worth 30 percent less than their nominal value.[69] At approximately the same time in Columbus, the notes of all three of these banks were valued at only 10 to 13 percent less than par value.[70]

This variance created complications for Apalachicola factors because the same money that was relatively worthless in Florida was preferred by the farmers of Georgia and Alabama. The Apalachicola factors knew if they did not pay the farmers in the money "current" (trading at par value) in Georgia, they would lose their share of the cotton trade to the towns upriver.[71] For that reason William G. Porter and Company of Apalachicola advertised they would make their advances on cotton in "Georgia money."[72]

Cotton merchants who lived on the river between the two cities were caught between two different rates. The frustration felt by J. W. Sutlive, a commission and forwarding merchant at Fort Gaines, Georgia, is evident by his announcement in the Apalachicola newspaper: "Managers of Steamboats on the Chattahoochee River, are desired to take notice, that any freight consigned to me, at Fort Gaines, will be paid in any money that is received at this place at par, without respect to its value in Columbus. Those boat-masters who will not accede to this, will not receive freight consigned to me, as I will not obligate to pay (what they call) bankable funds."[73]

The uneven state of the valley's currency at times strained the relations between cotton merchants and farmers. A merchant of Barbour County, Alabama, complained loudly that businessmen were being taken by farmers who sold their cotton for high prices in depreciated currency, and then expected local storeowners to accept the money at par value.[74]

Not only did merchants of the river valley have to contend with the changing values of their local currency, but also they had to deal with varying exchange rates outside their economic sphere. Just as world travelers today must exchange their currency when moving from one country to another, so did antebellum businessmen who traded outside their economic region.

The Columbus or Apalachicola commission merchant buying goods in the North had to purchase them in money current there. Consequently if he bought New York goods he had to pay for them in New York money. The local market reports included exchange rate tables that listed the purchase rates of the currency of various distant cities. The rates followed the course of trade and the law of supply and demand. In the summer when southern businessmen were in New York buying their stock of fall merchandise, the cost of obtaining New York money in the South was high. In the winter when northern money flowed into the South to purchase cotton, New York currency was easier to obtain and therefore sold at a discount there.[75]

When payments were due away from home, the debtor had the added responsibility of finding a means of transporting the payment to the creditor. The mails were notoriously unreliable and only used as a last resort. If one did not know an acquaintance who was about to travel to the place of indebtedness, private couriers or stage-coaches transported cash. If the debtor opted to send bank notes through the mail, he usually cut the bills in half, sending the second half only after hearing the first portion had arrived safely.[76]

A simpler means of repaying an outside debt involved the use of bills of exchange because their use allowed debts of individuals living at a distance from their creditors to be canceled without the transmission of money. A bill of exchange was a written order to one person to pay a third person a specified sum at a certain time and place. If the person to whom it was drawn "accepted" the bill by writing that word and his signature across the face of it, he was then legally bound to pay the sum on the specified date.

Bills of exchange could be used in two ways. If Mr. Smith owed Mr. Jones a sum of money, and Mr. White owed Mr. Smith another sum, Smith could cancel his debt with Jones by having White pay it. In this case the payment of funds was triangular.

In the cotton trade, there were usually four sides to the debt cancellation. If A in Columbus owed B in Apalachicola and C in Apalachicola owed D in Columbus, instead of A in Columbus sending money to B in Apalachicola and C in the latter place forwarding money to D in Columbus, A simply bought from D of the same city an order directing C in Apalachicola to pay his neighbor B. Again two debts had been canceled without the trans-mission of money.[77]

In addition to bills of exchange, antebellum entrepreneurs often used promissory notes for debt payment. These were simply written promises to pay someone a certain sum of money on a stated date.[78] Unlike the bill of exchange, the promissory note did not require the intervention of a third person. It was an order from A to pay B, as opposed to a bill of exchange, which was an order from A to B to pay C.[79]

At first blush it may seem that promissory notes were a means of getting into debt rather than a form of debt payment. It is true that it was the intent of the person originating the note, but in the course of trade within the valley both bills of exchange and promissory notes were used as currency for the payment of obligations. As an example, suppose A gives B a promissory note due in one year for services received. If B needs money to meet other liabilities before the year is up, he can endorse the note by signing his name on the back of it and sell it at a discount to a bank agent or someone else in a position to do so. The bank agent can then hold the note to maturity and collect the full value of the note or sell it again to a customer in need of some way to pay his obligations. If the latter course is taken, the note may change ownership several times before the year is up.

The same was true of a bill of exchange, which could be sold and resold at a discount either before or after the draft was accepted. Second-hand bills of exchange and promissory notes passed as currency in the valley as readily as coins or bank notes. The absence of an adequate currency mandated their use, but reusing drafts and notes in the course of trade had its complications. Imagine the repercussions when, after being traded several times, the person on whom the draft was initially made refused to honor his obligation. Unfortunately, newspaper advertisements like the following were a common sight to readers in Apalachicola and Columbus. "Notice— All persons are hereby cautioned against trading for a Promissory Note given by me to Samuel Gammon, for two hundred and fifty dollars ($250.00) due, I think, the 1st of March, 1845, endorsed by B. S. Hawley. The consideration for which said note was given having entirely failed, I shall not pay the same unless compelled by law."[80]

In addition to bills of exchange, promissory notes, coin, and bank notes, other financial paper circulated as currency in the region. Certificates of deposit[81] and checks on New York banks or other cities were bought and sold as if they were the actual cash represented by the paper. Because most southern debts were owed in New York, checks on New York banks were prized and, at times of the year, sold at a premium in the South.[82]

Cotton was often used to settle debts between distant points, especially when the exchange rate between them was exorbitant. Paris Tillinghast of Columbus once commented that cotton was a "good exchange" even though local bank notes were trading for notes outside the region at 15 to 18 percent discount. Apalachicola cotton factors routinely shipped cotton to their correspondents at other ports in payment of debts.[83]

The cotton dealer of the pre-war South was a combination merchant and banker. The price of money was as important to him as the going rate of cotton. With all the complications associated with antebellum currency conditions it is no wonder that businessmen spent most of their workday in keeping their ledgers. Very little money actually changed hands between a commission merchant and his clients on a daily basis. Instead, the merchant kept a running account of debits and credits that was usually settled only once a year, when the cotton was sold. For this reason, the clerk of a cotton firm was the most important and busiest employee of all, working thirteen to fifteen hours a day just to keep up with the paperwork.[84]

The currency conditions of the Apalachicola/Chattahoochee River valley resembled those of other developing regions of the antebellum South. The differences among the separate river economies were a matter of degrees. The Cotton South was not monolithic in the rate of its economic development. Conditions existing in the cotton economies of the Alabama River system to the west (whose seaport was Mobile) or the Savannah River system on the Atlantic Ocean to the east were not precisely mirrored in the waters flowing through the younger Apalachicola/Chattahoochee economy where financial institutions were relatively fewer and weaker and where regulations of three different state governments had a hand in complicating matters. Nevertheless, antebellum businessmen adapted to the particular monetary conditions they encountered, and, given the challenges they faced, were remarkably successful.

# 4

## *Cotton Banks*

HE ANTEBELLUM HISTORY OF THE VALLEY'S BANKING
institutions is a tale of extremes. These were years of
boom and bust, too many banks, then not enough. Government regulation was virtually nonexistent in the early years, then
overzealous (in the case of Alabama and Florida) in the latter. Cotton merchants complained loudly about high interest charges and
exchange rates, but these were the cost of doing business. Because
the transport of cotton from producer to consumer took several
months and because the producer did not wish to wait for his payment, a class of entrepreneurs developed that specialized in the
extension of commercial credit.

Difficulties arose in this undertaking because the South (indeed,
the entire nation) did not yet have a pool of liquid capital from
which to draw to finance commerce adequately. A national banking
system had yet to emerge from the wide array of "highly individu-
alistic" financial intermediaries.[1] Overcoming this fragmentation
in banking structure, as well as the dearth of capital, constituted
the local bankers' greatest challenges, and most of them in the
Apalachicola/Chattahoochee River valley would ultimately fail to
overcome these obstacles.

Banks of the early nineteenth century were primarily "banks of issue." They created credit by the circulation of their notes that promised to pay the bearer in an equivalent amount of specie (coin) on demand. Bank notes were more widely acceptable than the notes of an individual or a corporation because bank notes were issued by those who had more expertise in such matters and who had the combined resources of their stockholders backing them. As long as a bank maintained a reputation for redeeming its notes in specie on demand, its notes were valued, and they readily passed as money.[2]

Bankers were able to expand their operations beyond simply brokering the assets of their stockholders to a lender by the use of "fractional reserves." Because bankers knew that in normal times their creditors would not all cash in their bank notes on the same day, they reserved in their vaults only a fraction of the specie necessary to convert their outstanding notes. As long as the public had confidence in the bank, things ran smoothly. There was a tendency, however, for the banks to overextend themselves. Bankers were tempted to underestimate the specie reserves necessary to meet outstanding liabilities, for idle money collecting dust in the back room was not earning its keep.

In the twenty-five years following the War of 1812, most state banking charters required only from 12 to 50 percent of one's initial capital to be constituted in specie, with 20 percent being an average proportion.[3] Credit was needed so badly in developing areas that politicians wanted to do nothing that would hinder their establishment. Consequently, lawmakers were very lenient in setting minimum capital requirements before a bank could begin operations.

Once the banks opened their doors, further state regulation was negligible, and it was all too common for bankers to violate their charter's specie requirements because in this credit-starved region, producing bank notes was a much cheaper means of procuring credit than borrowing money from the wealthier Northeast. The public generally believed that any credit institution was better than none in a region developing at such a phenomenal pace.[4]

Recently, economic historians have been more sympathetic to the difficulties that bankers faced, and they have pointed out that some of their seemingly reckless practices had a positive, inflationary effect on the region by creating as much credit for the area's businessmen as was possible.[5] This observation is certainly true, for without the bankers, a cotton trade would never have developed in the Apalachicola/Chattahoochee River valley. Nevertheless, this frontier region suffered greatly by the retardation of its banking development, which prevented it from keeping pace with the other cotton-producing regions of the South.

During Andrew Jackson's presidency, banks were less apt to get into trouble by their overextension, for they were operating in an expanding economy. With every passing year it seemed the amount of money in circulation increased. The volume of the money supply, mostly in the form of specie-backed state bank notes, was directly proportionate to the amount of specie circulating in the country. The combined effects of a rise in silver imports from Mexico plus a decreased outflow of specie to Asia meant that more specie found its way into bank vaults. In the prosperous 1830s there was simply more specie around with which to back up the banks' notes. As money became easier to come by, bankers became looser with it. When people spent more, prices inflated, creating more opportunities for investment. As the U.S. government paid off its deficit, English investors' confidence in American securities grew, and they became eager to finance American commerce and development. The economy blossomed.[6]

As long as English banking houses continued to extend credit to American importers and exporters, everything went well. But the American economy was so utterly dependent on English credit to finance trade that any disruption of that credit to America was bound to have disastrous effects. In 1837 when the Bank of England, believing that a British specie drain was attributable to an unfavorable balance of trade with America, curtailed its discounts of American paper, the few giant private banking houses followed their lead. As credit tightened, American businessmen quickly encountered a surge in interest rates and a corresponding plummet in cotton prices since most sales were dependent on the availability of credit. When the price of cotton fell, merchants holding debts secured by cotton found them to be uncollectable. As merchants failed, the banks they owed money to also fell into trouble. A general panic ensued.[7]

As more and more note holders demanded specie of the banks that issued them, the fractional reserves of every bank were not sufficient to meet liabilities. Because there was no central banking system in America, there was no place for the banks to turn in order to liquidate their assets quickly. The nation's banks were forced to suspend the redemption of their notes in specie. This action created "a free market for notes in terms of specie."[8] The value of local bank notes fell relative to their value in specie. Southern businessmen holding local bank notes but needing specie or foreign money to meet their debts in New York or England encountered exorbitant exchange rates. In order to resume redemption, banks were forced to reduce their notes-to-specie ratio. As bankers retired a large portion of their notes, the money supply contracted. Except for a brief recovery in 1838, American business was paralyzed by a crippling depression that lasted from 1837 to 1842.[9]

The banks in Columbus, Georgia, suspended specie payments for the majority of time between 1837 and 1842.[10] Just as specie redemption was suspended, the cost of exchange with the North soared drastically. Economic conditions in the valley snowballed as consumers found their infirmity ever worsening. The price of upland cotton in the New York market dipped down to as low as five cents per pound in 1842.[11]

Every businessman who even tangentially dealt in cotton felt the sting of this economic blow. Not only had they less income to pay their debts with, but the amount they owed outsiders increased dramatically relative to what they had borrowed because of the one-sided exchange rate. Buyers who needed New York money to pay northern debts found a relative depreciation in local currency of 15 to 18 percent.[12]

All over the valley men were embarrassed at not being able to repay their loans. One Columbus merchant who owed money in North Carolina found the exchange rate against him was 15 percent "without a corresponding difference in the prices of what we give for the currency here."[13] A well-to-do Columbus man wrote, "the few who have any credit can only return it by not attempting to use it." His friends were "in the fashionable language of the day . . . 'used up' . . . they may recover but for my life I can't see how."[14] He learned that things were just as bad on the Alabama side of the river.

There, in Henry County, the people formally asked the sheriff to resign because he had auctioned off farms to satisfy creditors. Acting collectively, they "unanimously refused to bid for any property he offers at his sales."[15] A Marianna, Florida, man declared, "Certainly . . . there never was such a time of suffering for the want of money as now exists."[16]

Merchants faced the impossible choice of paying the exorbitant price of exchange and going broke in the process or ruining their credit rating by refusal to pay. The newspaper reported the merchants were "suffering daily and hourly on account of the derangement in the currency. They are making heavy sacrifices to preserve their credit, and we fear they cannot long do it, unless the Banks shall come forward and meet their liabilities. In such a time as this, there ought to pervade in every bosom, a spirit of accommodation and kindness, and every man ought to be willing to make some sacrifice to aid his creditors."[17]

The banks blamed their inability to pay their note holders on those who could not repay their bank loans.[18] Columbus merchants threatened to sue the banks if they did not sell northern money at reasonable rates.[19] When their threats were unheeded they appealed to the Georgia legislature. Because the banks were in violation of Georgia law by not redeeming in specie, state authorities eventually placed the Columbus banks in receivership.[20]

Columbus merchants blamed the depreciation of their currency on the bank's inability to redeem their notes in coin. "No class of our citizens is more lavishly censured than those who preside over our banking institutions. . . . the impression prevails universally, that they have willingly contributed to bring upon the community the present exorbitant system of exchange. . . . As soon . . . as the specie payments were suspended, exchange rose immediately to an exorbitant rate."[21] It is a "matter of history," complained another, "that immediately after . . . [the banks suspended specie payments] Exchange rose from 3 to 18 per cent. premium."[22]

Like these two commentators, most people believed the exchange rate was tied to the banks' ability to redeem their notes in specie. Actually the exorbitant exchange rate with the North was related to export-import balances. Now that the export of cotton failed to cover the cost of imports, "exchange rose to a premium and bank currencies declined to a corresponding discount."[23]

Bankers were certainly guilty of aggravating the fluctuations in the antebellum economy. "They offered credit liberally in recovery and boom when their specie reserves seemed high. Then as specie flowed out because of . . . an unfavorable balance of trade, they tried desperately to maintain their reserves by stringent contraction."[24] But because their issue was based on a metallic standard and the availability of gold and silver was determined by external economic forces, they were as subject to circumstances beyond their control as the cotton growers were.[25]

This is not to say that all banks were blameless. The fact that the Columbus banks were never able to resume specie payments testifies to their mismanagement. The operation of the Planters and Mechanics Bank is a particular example of malfeasance. Its 1837 charter required it to have a paid-in capital of $250,000 in specie before opening its doors. This money was never raised, but the stockholders opened for business without it, intending to be its preferred borrowers and to take advantage of the nationwide suspension of specie redemption.

While banks all over the country suspended specie payments, the Planters and Mechanics Bank commenced operations. Throughout its existence, this bank never redeemed its notes in specie.[26] In 1841 it reported having $178,650 of its bank notes in circulation. Individual deposits (subject to withdrawal on demand) totaled $114,185. To offset these combined liabilities totaling $292,835 the bank reported it held only $15,665 in gold and silver coin, yielding a ratio of immediate liabilities to specie of over twenty to one.[27] Even so, certain locals continued to defend the bank's management. Years later the *Columbus Enquirer*, a qualified supporter of all local banks, defended this bank's actions by arguing that unlike the other Georgia banks that had issued notes promising redemption in specie but then reneged, the Planters and Mechanics Bank had never deceived the public because it opened as a suspended bank.[28]

The Chattahoochee Railroad and Banking Company of Columbus was another casualty of the depression. When the books were opened for inspection at the time of its failure, it was found to have only $118.58 in "cash" to offset $199,960 worth of notes in circulation. Even though it was illegal for a Georgia bank to deal in cotton,[29] the Chattahoochee Bank admitted it had a "cotton account" of $90,341.60. The bank had bought cotton for speculation and had lost its wager. Now that the price of cotton had dipped, most of this amount represented a loss. Additionally there were almost twenty-nine thousand dollars in overdrafts of favored customers. As the bank wound up its affairs it appears the insiders sucked off what assets they could. In the last three months of its troubled existence the amount of the bank's loans doubled.[30] Further scrutiny of the bank records revealed "the President, Cashier and Directors, all combined, owed the Bank, at the time it failed, the snug sum of $85,706.14."[31]

Irresponsible bankers such as these blamed others for their inability to meet their liabilities. They claimed they had no choice but to suspend specie redemption because they alleged that individuals had been "traversing the country, in every direction, searching for Columbus notes, and paying a high premium for them, in order to draw specie" purposely to ruin them.[32] Another pro-bank argument blamed the dearth of banks in Alabama and Florida for increasing the demand for specie at Columbus.[33]

In an effort to weather the depression, even reputable banks curtailed loans. If they were ever to resume specie payments they had to decrease their notes in circulation relative to onhand assets. But this contraction of credit crippled all business, especially that not related to the cotton trade. Paris Tillinghast moved to Columbus in the nadir of the depression. He wrote his brother to explain the impossibility of arranging credit for his mercantile operations: "There are not many in business that are under any obligations to

Banks here. I mean those who buy goods abroad & sell them here. The Banks discounting no notes for them by way of aid to business. What do they care for them? Since we have been here I cannot learn that the Banks do any other business except in advancing money on cotton & making the Interest & Exchange out of the circulation of their notes."[34]

Downriver in Florida, banking conditions were similar. The largest of Apalachicola's depression era banks was actually a branch of St. Augustine's Southern Life Insurance and Trust Company. It was "empowered to sell insurance, make loans, import, export, issue currency, develope timber lands, discount money, etc."[35] A St. Augustine newspaper declared it had " 'every power except that of killing Indians.' "[36]

This New York–based bank was created in order to circulate the notes of an associated New York bank as far away from the North as possible.[37] Regardless of its origins, Apalachicola cotton factors were glad to get a bank there. They argued that if the proprietors of the bank were nonresidents, they would not be its borrowers and, therefore, the entire banking capital would be used for local business operations.[38]

After 10 percent of the total stock had been paid in, the Southern Life opened its doors in November 1835. The Apalachicola branch, the largest office of the concern, opened the next year.[39] By 1836 five hundred thousand dollars had been paid in as stock in the bank, most of it going into New York banks at the credit of the Southern Life.[40] According to its charter the bank could not issue more bank notes than its paid-in capital, and it could not refuse to redeem its notes in specie.[41]

When the Panic of 1837 set in and banks all over the country suspended specie redemption, the firm secured permission from the Florida legislative council to do likewise. With the onset of the depression, the New York stockholders found it difficult to continue meeting the installments of their stock subscription. While claiming they were opening their books in order to counter criticisms that the stock was not owned locally, they tendered one million dollars' worth of their stock for sale at Apalachicola. This stock was to be issued in exchange for 8 percent mortgages on Florida land. The mortgage giver was then eligible to borrow three-fifths of the par value of his stock by pledging it back to the bank.[42]

The selling agent who traveled through west and middle Florida told the prospective buyers that the twice annual dividends of 5 percent would more than cover the 8 percent cost of their mortgages.[43] A man who later sued the bank scoffed at "this generous desire of the Wall Street speculators to share with the country gentlemen of Florida the 10 per cent dividends—and also their responsibility for the unpaid portions of their stock."[44]

Nevertheless, subscribers of stock in the Apalachicola branch soon took advantage of their position as favored customers. Loans to these stockholders far exceeded the three-fifths of their mortgage value stipulated in the charter. The commission business of Hiram Nourse and Company received loans worth twice its purchased stock value, and all the other stockholders of the Apalachicola office except one received loans equal to the full amount of their stock subscription.[45]

Many Floridians, including the governor, reviled the bank who "'waves the flag of its displeasure' over those who demand the specie to which its currency purports to be equivalent, and dispenses its favors only and largely to its friends."[46] Indeed, the bank's operations did deteriorate into "gross favoritism for a few at the expense of the many."[47] It irresponsibly discounted a large number of loans backed only by personal security and allowed cotton merchants to overdraw their accounts excessively. In 1840 and 1841, the overdrafts at Apalachicola equaled over twenty thousand dollars.[48]

Banks, like the Southern Life in Apalachicola, indirectly financed the cotton trade in two ways. A merchant (or a planter with the endorsement of his factor) might receive an advance from the bank by tendering his promissory note. The note was secured with cotton, and by the time the loan fell due, it was hoped the cotton would be sold at a price sufficient to repay it.

Alternately, the bank might "discount" a bill of exchange that had been generated also by the sale of cotton. The term "discounting" came from the practice of charging the customer in advance for the use of the bank's money. The banker discounted a promissory note or bill of exchange by deducting the interest charge at the initiation of the loan so that a person borrowing one thousand dollars at 10 percent interest actually received only nine hundred dollars.[49] In either case, the banker bought the bill of exchange or promissory note from cotton factors at a discount corresponding to the amount of interest the paper would earn if it were held to maturity.[50]

The banker could then either hold the paper until it was due and collect the interest or resell it to a banker elsewhere that had a customer owing money in the place where the paper originated. For that reason, the Columbus banks routinely bought bills of exchange on Apalachicola, which they could resell to Georgians owing money in Apalachicola.[51] When they resold them to the public it was said they "sold exchange."

The Southern Life Bank of Apalachicola advanced thousands of dollars to cotton holders in anticipation of the staple's sale through the discounting of either promissory notes or bills of exchange. This was a highly speculative practice for the bank because if the price of cotton suddenly bottomed as it did in 1837 the farmer could not repay the loan and its collateral security was worthless. In January 1841 when cotton prices were at their nadir, the Apalachicola office of the Southern Life had outstanding advances on cotton amounting to $52,163.42 in addition to its twenty thousand dollars' worth of overdrafts made by cotton merchants.[52] Most of this debt was never repaid.

The most lucrative banking service was probably the business of "exchange." Initially, the term denoted the business of buying and selling nonlocal money for trade purposes. When an Apalachicola commission merchant owed money to a New Orleans merchant for purchasing a quantity of groceries, the Apalachicola merchant had to pay this debt in money passing at par in New Orleans. The Apalachicola factor, then, had either to purchase New Orleans bank notes and send them to New Orleans, or to buy a bill of exchange on New Orleans for the amount owed. In either case, he went to his banker to buy "exchange."

The legitimate principal behind the bank's charging "exchange" rested on the cost of transporting money between the two cities. But in actuality funds were never physically moved; one payment of debt canceled another.

Actually, the exchange charge was commonly used to bypass the states' usury laws that set a maximum rate of interest on bank loans. When the bank discounted a bill of exchange, it charged the legal rate of interest plus a percentage for "exchange." The fee was actually a commission charge. When the interest and exchange rates were combined, it caused the actual interest rate to be as high as 37 percent.[53] The Southern Life Bank of Apalachicola charged an additional 2 percent above the legal interest rate for drawing on its New York office and 15 percent or higher on drafts of other banks.[54] Even if a customer offered to sell a local bill of exchange, the bank often required him to alter it so as to make it payable in another location before discounting it and charging exchange.[55]

Prospective lenders who offered their promissory note paid the same charge. Exchange was added to the other costs of the loan "whenever money was to be paid in a different place from that in which it was loaned."[56] No matter that the customer stood in the Apalachicola office of the bank requesting money to be repaid there; the bank could make the loan *appear* to involve two locations by refusing to accept a promissory note payable at home. The bank required the lender to sign a note payable on a certain date at the office of a correspondent bank in another city. The bank charged the customer "exchange" in advance for having to collect the money in another city when the loan was due. This fee was far more than the actual costs of negotiating funds between the two cities. Typically a loan was made to run six months or less. Every time the loan was renewed an additional commission was added.[57]

To facilitate these transactions, as well as that of the genuine exchange of currency between commercial points, the Southern Life kept balances in correspondent banks in New York, Charleston, and Savannah, and these banks had reciprocating balances in Apalachicola. In order to maintain a deposit account away from home, the bank bought cotton and shipped it to the other ports where it was sold and the proceeds deposited in the correspondent bank.[58] This practice had the deleterious effect of putting the banks in the business of cotton speculation, which made the price of cotton more volatile. When cotton was locally in large demand for the payment of exchange, heavy bidding for the staple caused the price to go up artificially above its value in other markets.[59] In that case there was sure to be a loss when the cotton was resold. Some banks also dealt in cotton merely for speculation.

Apalachicola's Southern Life company was so active in cotton dealing it was known as "the cotton bank."[60] Many believed these cotton ventures caused its demise. The bank committee of the Florida legislature strongly chastised Southern Life for this practice, saying, "The cotton speculations the bank has engaged in directly by purchase of, or indirectly by loans or advances . . . afford themselves full cause for [their] embarrassments."[61]

The bank was indeed in trouble, but its cotton speculations were only partly to blame. The bank's own statement of this year indicates the bank had a circulation of $72,643. To back up its notes, it had "specie funds" (the notes of other specie-paying banks) worth $7,998. Thus the bank had issued notes worth almost ten times its ability to repay them. In this, the twilight of its existence, it had no gold or silver whatsoever in its vaults.[62]

In 1842 it turned its assets over to a Tallahassee law firm for collection. As it was born, so did it die. The debts of the bank were divided into two classes: those funds borrowed in the North were to be repaid first; Florida depositors and note holders had to wait in line for any recompense.[63] In 1844 the Apalachicola office of the Southern Life was auctioned off to pay three local creditors.[64]

All the original banking institutions of the Apalachicola/Chattahoochee River valley had failed by 1844. Their demography was typical of that of other underdeveloped areas of the antebellum period, which were characterized by one banking historian as having "high birth rates and high death rates."[65]

As banks failed, governments overreacted in their attempted remedy. Lawmakers' two most common reactions were to prohibit banking altogether or to make banking regulation more stringent.

Alabama and Florida were among a group of seven states, two territories, and the District of Columbia that followed the former course, while Georgia took the latter.[66]

Congress allowed no further banks to be chartered while Florida was a territory.[67] Florida's 1845 state constitution was written by an anti-bank faction and was so strict that no banks were chartered under it for a decade. Banks were limited by it to operate only as places of " 'exchange, discount and deposit.' "[68] They could no longer raise credit through the issue of bank notes because the state restricted their issue to not more than twice their reserved specie.

This situation left Apalachicola in the ludicrous condition of being the largest commercial center in Florida with no currency of its own. During most of the period between 1840 and 1860, the port was dependent on Georgia bank notes as its medium of exchange. In 1842 a senator from Calhoun County, Florida, just upriver from Apalachicola pleaded with the senate banking committee: "You are aware of the condition of the currency, and of the want of proper trading facilities of the people in our section of the Territory. It is important that we have a bank whose bills should be on a par with those of the Columbus banks."[69] But this was not to be. Even after the restrictions were eased somewhat in 1853, Apalachicola never had another locally chartered bank in the antebellum period.[70]

Obviously, just because banks were legislatively banned did not mean that banking operations were suspended. Apalachicola was a vital commercial port that required currency and credit. To fill the void left by the failed banks, agencies of distant banks took root in the Florida sand. As early as 1840 the Bank of Columbus had an agency in Apalachicola.[71] In 1846 there were four foreign bank agencies in town, and by 1850 there were eight.[72] The *Southern Business Directory* of 1854 listed seven local commission merchants who acted as agents of foreign banks as a sideline to their primary business of marketing cotton.[73] The banking capital afforded a bank agent gave these men a distinct advantage in marketing cotton.

Foreign banks saw in Apalachicola the opportunity to simplify their exchange operations and circulate their bank notes farther from home. It was advantageous for an upriver Georgia bank to have an agency in Apalachicola so that exchange with the port city could be easily effected. This was also an excellent way for a bank in South Carolina located out of Apalachicola's normal trade channels to circulate its notes, making their course back to the issuer for redemption more difficult. Foreign banks were also out of the jurisdiction of Florida law, allowing them to use whatever business tactics they chose.

Customers in Apalachicola found there were drawbacks to doing business with these foreign agencies. For instance, agencies were only open during the peak of the cotton marketing season. The Apalachicola cotton firm of Austin and Long had to make other arrangements for borrowing money in October 1850 because the "Bank Agencies are not underweigh [*sic*] here yet."[74]

Because there were no local banks in Apalachicola, the foreign agencies often became the scapegoat for the foibles of the national economy. The Apalachicola newspaper editor claimed that since the agencies there were controlled by banks far removed, they had no regard for what the local businessmen needed. The editor charged that whenever a financial panic arose, the parent banks shut down their agencies there but continued their operations at home, leaving Apalachicolans without means to pay their creditors.

Most bank agencies concentrated on the large and lucrative exchange business necessary for a cotton port. The chaotic state of the nation's inequivalent currency created splendid opportunities for specialists who by keeping abreast of the worth of hundreds of bank notes and checks could make a handsome profit.[75] Scores of advertisements like the following selling exchange appeared in the Apalachicola newspapers:

CHECKS!—Checks on New York and New Orleans for sale at the Agency of the Augusta Insurance & Banking Co.

CHECKS ON NEW YORK—For sale at the agency of the Mechanics Bank.

EXCHANGE—Bought and sold, by WM. G. PORTER, Agent Bank Brunswick.

DOUBLOONS AND SOVEREIGNS—for sale by JAS. KEL-
LOGG, Agent.

AMERICAN GOLD—For sale in sums to suit purchasers, by
WM. G. PORTER & CO.[76]

Although it appears from their advertisements that dealing in
exchange was the main function of Apalachicola's private bankers,
they no doubt carried on all the other banking tasks except creating
bank notes, such as accepting deposits and making loans and collections.

The business of collections dovetailed with that of dealing in
exchange. A businessman in another city who owned a bill of exchange coming due in Apalachicola could deposit it with an Apalachicola banker so that the drawee could pay it there. This was a
convenience to both the drawer and drawee, and it allowed a small
profit to the banker. The Bank of Columbus, Georgia, scattered
eleven agents throughout the valley at all the major communities on
the river, including the port city. They advertised that collections
made by the "mother bank" at Columbus would be made without
charge, and at the agencies "subject to the charge customary at
points where they are located."[77]

Apalachicola's banking businesses were meager compared to the
volume of cotton that came through the port. Although most historians have pointed to the shallow depth of water in Apalachicola Bay
as the reason why the port eventually lost out to rival ports, the lack
of banking capital was more to blame.[78] Apalachicola was the only
American cotton port that did not have at least one strong local
bank. In 1845, L. F. E. Dugas, a newcomer to Apalachicola, complained that negotiating money there posed the greatest difficulty in
buying cotton in that market.[79]

Upriver from Apalachicola, the state of banking was equally debilitating. Alabama's experiment with a state-owned bank was such
a failure that no new banks were chartered there after the depression. The people of the Alabama side of the Chattahoochee were
without a native bank for most of the period from 1840 to 1860.

Following the depression Georgia banks were allowed to exist, but lawmakers there insisted on more assurances of their banks' solvency. Prior to 1837, state banking charters had been granted only to the legislators' friends. With the financial panic of 1837 highlighting the corruption of these now-failed banks, Georgia, like sixteen other states passed a "free banking" law in 1838.

The lawmakers' goal was to allow banking to continue but with safeguards to its depositors and noteholders. By this reform legislation, a state charter was no longer necessary. Anyone was "free" to engage in banking after depositing approved securities worth the value of the bank's note issues with the state. Free banking, however, "was only as safe as the securities deposited against the notes."[80] It was only when many of these new banks defaulted on their notes that it was discovered that most of the securities pledged were worthless.[81]

Most of the Columbus banks that operated under the free banking law were managed only slightly more conservatively than those that succumbed in the depression. The major difference now was that the banks were again riding a growing economy. The discovery of gold in California in the late 1840s caused the volume of specie in circulation in the nation to leap from a value of 120 million dollars in 1848 to 260 million dollars in 1856.[82] As in the 1830s, an increase in the amount of specie in the country's bank vaults meant a corresponding rise in the amount of specie-backed bank notes. There were still failures and fraud in the inflationary 1850s, but the public's attention on the banks was not so riveted as it had been when the economy was sour.

John Winter's Bank of St. Mary's moved to Columbus in 1843 to fill the void left by the failure of all the depression-era banks.[83] Winter's conservative management of this bank during the rest of the decade exemplifies the management of all the survivors of the depression. Statements for the years 1844 to 1849 show the bank's ratio of immediate liabilities (deposits and notes in circulation) to specie was approximately three to one.[84] This was considered a very safe margin of exposure. With the return of high cotton prices in 1849, the lessons learned in the depression must have faded from Winter's memory. In 1850 his immediate liabilities jumped to six times his reserved specie.[85] Two years later the bank failed owing $350,000 in outstanding notes.[86]

Like the Southern Life company at Apalachicola, the Bank of St. Mary's lent money to cotton holders in advance of its sale even though this practice violated Georgia law.[87] In the period from 1844 to 1850 total cotton advances fluctuated from a low of twenty-five hundred dollars in 1846 to a high of $45,500 in April 1850. The average amount yearly lent using cotton as collateral was approximately twenty-seven thousand dollars.[88]

Funding the cotton trade was the primary business of most Columbus banks. Whether they adequately met the demands made on them by cotton dealers is not known, but men in other businesses complained of insufficient credit. Paris Tillinghast wrote his brother on a familiar theme in 1854 saying, "There are periods here, in the City of Columbus, where no money is to be raised by fair ordinary means; when credit, except to a very few is without existence, sympathy extinct."[89] At the time he wrote this comment there were no local banks in Columbus; only the agencies of banks of other Georgia cities operated there.[90]

All during the two decades prior to the Civil War, the banks of Savannah and Augusta, Georgia, and Charleston, South Carolina, retained agencies in Columbus.[91] Of these, only the Bank of Brunswick (of Augusta) published annual statements in the Columbus newspapers, which aid us in ascertaining the quality of its management. Although the accounts of the Columbus agency are not completely separated from the parent bank, it is possible to deduce that the Columbus office had a correspondent for the making of exchange at Apalachicola; that it financed the sale of cotton by advancing on it in Columbus approximately $6,500 in 1847 and $13,500 the following year; and that the specie on reserve there approximated the aggregate of its cotton advances.[92]

If the other agencies in town followed this sound principle of maintaining resources to cover obligations, then the agencies' critics were in error when they accused them of siphoning off the specie of Columbus to the cities that sponsored them. In 1846 a merchant wrote, "Can we even expect to have a specie currency, while we have but one [local] Bank to bring it here and three [agencies] to send it out?"[93] He was referring to the fact that, by law, agencies could not issue their own bank notes, although they did serve to keep the notes of the parent bank in circulation.

Other criticisms included the charge that the people of Columbus were given as currency bank notes not redeemable locally, which amounted to having non-specie paying bills. Columbusites took the risk by accepting the currency in trade, but the profits went to the shareholders of the Atlantic coastal cities. Additionally, agencies of out-of-state banks were not bound by Georgia bank laws or taxation.[94]

All these charges, as well as those directed at Apalachicola agencies, represent the oversimplified logic of a frustrated populace who blamed the banks for the inadequacies of the national financial structure. Bank agencies may have been profitable affairs for their absentee stockholders, but they also aided the business community of the river valley by providing the only extant credit facilities. Their management could hardly have been worse than the home-grown variety.

The bank agent limited his loans primarily to cotton transactions. Paris Tillinghast complained of this fact in 1855. "Bank agencies here afford no relief to those who want money to pay debts. All their advances are on cotton."[95] The previous year he complained similarly that the bank agents "will discount a few notes; but very seldom. They generally say they do not do such business but they do it for a few; where they think their Interest is concerned particularly."[96]

Columbus radically needed another source of money for the discounting of notes. Unchartered "private bankers" filled this niche. These men specialized in discounting notes, but for this service they charged rates far exceeding the legal bank rates. Occasionally they bought advertisements such as this: "A few thousand dollars to loan on good personal or collateral security. Inquire at S. R. Bonner's General Agency Office."[97] In 1860 there were three private bankers in Albany, five in Columbus, three in Apalachicola, and two in Marianna, Florida.[98]

The general public seemed to distrust these men even more than the corporate bankers. Apalachicola's *Commercial Advertiser* ran a series of articles entitled "Usury: The Evil and The Remedy." Its author called attention to the unfairness of a financial system that permitted a few bank directors to receive loans at 6 percent when one not so privileged was compelled to walk farther down the street to a private concern and submit to as high as 36 percent.[99] A Columbus resident calling himself "One of the People" accused the private bankers of being the loudest detractors of corporate banks, for if the latter were pressed to redeem an unusual amount of their notes in specie, the money market would tighten, allowing the private "shaver" to charge a higher rate for the use of his money.[100]

The complaints about the valley's banking businesses were naturally at their loudest during the depression. By 1844 the worst of the financial upheaval was over, although the price of cotton did not fully rebound until 1846.[101] The national economy grew steadily, though unevenly, throughout the 1850s.

The return to prosperity in the last antebellum decade encouraged the growth of "country banks."[102] Albany, Georgia, at the head of navigation on the Flint River, got its first local bank in 1856.[103] Boosters in Fort Gaines, Georgia, on the Chattahoochee, promoted a bank there, but they were unable to get it past the Democrats in the state legislature who were rabidly anti-bank.[104] The regional cotton marketing town of Eufaula, Alabama, did not have a local bank from the time of the demise of the Irwinton Bridge Bank in 1844 until the establishment of the Eastern Bank of Alabama in 1858.[105] Two years earlier, the Southern Bank of Georgia opened in Bainbridge, on the lower Flint River, but it did not survive the Panic of 1857.[106]

The cause of the financial crisis in the autumn of 1857 was unrelated to the cotton trade (it had more to do with railroad overexpansion than anything else), yet the Cotton South was drawn into the panic when New York banks suspended specie payments. Occurring in the fall just as the cotton moved to market, the panic quickly spread to southern banks whose business was so intertwined with New York banks that most were forced to suspend as well.[107] However, unlike the 1837 crisis, this one was short-lived. New York banks rebounded within a few months, and most Georgia banks were able to resume specie redemption by the end of 1858.[108]

In the midst of the general economic optimism of the 1850s, the Panic of 1857 surprised southern businessmen much as the financial affliction of twenty years before.[109] Again the exchange rate between South and North soared. Columbus merchants, using the same logic they had employed two decades earlier, appealed to the state legislature to mandate decent exchange rates with the North.[110]

Those who had not witnessed the previous depression seem to have taken the situation more philosophically. Writing from his office above the Bank of Columbus, a young businessman likened his love life to the financial woes of the times: "I rec'd a very . . . indifferent, *wish-I-hadn't-to-give-it*, sort of Kiss through her veil from Cousin Annie, (I could but think her pretty rosy lips had under the pressure of the times suspended specie payments and substituted a fluctuating medium which bore upon one side at least a counterfeit impression. In truth I never expect to make another deposit while the bills of that very interesting institution are under so dark a cloud)" [emphasis his].[111]

Although valley residents felt the financial contraction, most Columbus lenders were strong enough to weather the crisis. The Bank of Columbus was the only locally owned bank in operation at the time of the panic.[112] William H. Young, its president, had opened the office the year before, using the capital he had assumed as a cotton commission merchant in Apalachicola.[113] The bank's statement in the spring of 1857 demonstrates its sound position going into the recession, and this bank never suspended paying specie for its notes as did most other banks in the country.[114] The 1857 condition of the five foreign agencies located in Columbus is not known, but agencies of the banks of Charleston, Augusta, and Savannah were still in existence in 1860.[115] Because the 1857 recession was not tied to the price of cotton, which remained firm because of a short crop, the recession was short-lived in the South. By 1860 Paris Tillinghast was able to report excellent financial conditions in the valley.

On the eve of the Civil War, the northern end of the river valley was thriving. Banks were a requisite for economic growth. Georgia law had fostered the creation of banks that, in turn, created the credit that Columbus businessmen needed. When times were good, bankers aided the local economy by expanding the money supply and offering credit to those in need of it. Over the years, most of the local bankers had been guilty of playing fast and loose, and they had failed when the health of the economy they operated in sickened. Yet these men were no different from businessmen of any sort in any part of the American frontier during the Jacksonian Age. They were all aggressive "men on the make" who seized the numerous opportunities to earn their fortunes in a fast-paced era of development in which the rules of play had not yet been codified.

By 1860 Columbus had become one of the South's most important industrial sites. Factory building was an expensive enterprise that took capital and credit. In spite of a wildly fluctuating national economy and the many mistakes they made, the financial intermediaries of Columbus had been able to support the city's expansion, while simultaneously servicing the important cotton and grocery trade.

But down on the coast, there was a noticeable difference. Without a bank of its own, Apalachicola was not keeping pace with other cities. The foreign bank agencies and private bankers were apparently able to meet the needs of the cotton trade by providing a local money market where the bills of exchange and promissory notes generated by the cotton dealers could be translated into ready cash. This was, of course, a vital function in a cotton town devoted to the export trade. But there was no vision of the future for Apalachicola merchants who continued to concentrate on the export business to the exclusion of any other form of commerce. The cotton trade itself was injured in the long run by the paucity of credit that was needed to finance the improvement of the river and harbor. It seems that even an irresponsible bank would have been better for Apalachicola than no bank at all.

# 5

## *Financing the Cotton Trade*

PANNING THE ATLANTIC OCEAN FROM LONDON TO NEW
York and stretching down into the Old South, an intricate
credit structure underpinned the burgeoning cotton trade.
In this era of slow transportation, it was necessary for the cotton to
be financed while it was in transit from the grower to the buyer.
Because the South lacked the liquid capital necessary to finance its
own major export, a long and convoluted chain of finance accom-
panied the cotton bales out of the South and into the world market.

As David L. Cohn has said, "The antebellum South was not rich
in banks, and its banks were not rich."[1] Most southern capital was
tied up in land and slaves. By discounting bills of exchange and
promissory notes local banks performed a vital role in the cotton
trade's financial network, but they were not the final source of
southern credit.

Ultimately credit did not originate in the South at all, but in
England whose giant textile industry fed ravenously on southern
cotton. London's money market was the strongest in the world, and
it was capable of discounting all the foreign bills of exchange that
were generated by the textile industry.

This stream of credit from London made its way to the South
circuitously. The South did not require a steady source of sterling

exchange (that is, bills of exchange drawn against England) because its exports to England far outweighed its demand for British manufactured goods. If England and the South had traded directly, ships coming to cotton ports would have had to come in ballast, a condition that was prohibitively expensive. New York grew to eminence as the country's major port by rerouting southern products and English financial resources through its facilities. In fact, it was so successful at this rerouting that by 1860 two-thirds of American imports and one-third of its exports passed through its harbor, and New York had become the financial capital of the South.

As in any business, the availability of credit was the most vital element in conducting a successful cotton concern. With their strategic position at the apex of the cotton triangle, New Yorkers were able to tie into the English money market. This connection allowed them to extend credit to the southern commission merchant who, in turn, could offer the same to southern planters. Through New York commission merchants, southern factors were able to buy the goods their customers needed on credit, and they were able to provide cash payments to cotton growers in advance of the sale of their cotton. This linkage, however, put southern cotton traders in a vulnerable position within the marketing network, for they relied on financial sources beyond their control in order to extend a second-hand credit to their customers.

The detour from Europe to the South through New York and back again complicated financial affairs. Because exchange on New York was easily marketable in the South where it was needed to pay debts in the North, and sterling exchange was rarely needed since the South purchased most of its manufactured goods (even European ones) from New York, Apalachicola commission merchants found it necessary to draw exchange on New York even when consigning cotton to be sold in England. New Yorkers, in turn, drew on London for reimbursement.[2]

This chain of finance that followed the cotton on its way from the Georgia farm to the English mill was affected by a series of advances. At harvest time the cotton farmers sold their cotton to their storekeeper.[3] Planters and inland storekeepers who dealt in greater volumes consigned their cotton to a commission merchant at the coast who offered to pay them an advance of from two-thirds to three-fourths of the sale price for their cotton before the merchants found a buyer for it. This advance might be paid in the form of cash or a promissory note, but the most common way in the Apalachicola hinterland was by using a bill of exchange.

In this case the planter or country storekeeper drew a bill of exchange on his commission merchant which directed the factor to pay the planter the money for his cotton within a specified time. The planter or storeowner then took this draft to the local bank, which discounted it. The object was for the planter to be able to receive the proceeds from the sale of his cotton without waiting for the eventual sale. The commission merchant intended to sell the planter's cotton before the draft became due so that he would have the funds to pay the draft.

Funds for paying the planter did not originate with his commission merchant, but with the actual buyer of the cotton. Commission houses in New York and England sold the cotton for the southern factor to a textile mill or another speculator, or they bought cotton on their own account for speculation. At the time of shipment to them, the northerners paid an advance to the southern commission merchant in the form of a sixty-day sight bill. This bill required the draft to be paid sixty days after it had been accepted. The northern and/or European firms then usually had sufficient time to receive and sell the cotton in time to honor this draft. Since the mails were dependent on relatively irregular and slow-sailing ships, twice that amount of time might actually pass between the drawing of the bill and its due date. In the meantime the southern commission merchant had funds with which to pay the planter's or inland storekeeper's draft by discounting (selling at a discount) the second draft to a local banker or broker. One who discounted a bill of exchange was said to be "buying exchange."[4]

If a New York house advanced money to the southern merchant before reconsigning the cotton to an English commission house, it drew a bill on the English house, which then drew on the textile mill.[5] The New York firm sold this draft in the New York money market and used the proceeds to cover its draft to the southern factor. The number of bills drawn for the sale of one lot of cotton was virtually limitless depending on the number of middlemen involved.

Eventually the cotton was sold to a textile factory. If the price of cotton at its final sale remained firm, the cotton grower received the balance of the money owed him (the difference between the advance and the sale price). If the price in the Liverpool market fell while the cotton was in transit, the English commission merchant had to fall back on the person who sold it to him and so on until the "reclamation" came back to the grower who had to pay his creditor in order to settle his account. Reclamations were also instigated when the cotton weighed less or was of an inferior quality than had been claimed by the shipper.[6]

Often these proceedings produced hard feelings, if not litigation, between the grower and the English commission merchant. When the New York firm of Pillot and Le Barbier consigned 202 bales of a Columbus man's cotton to a Liverpool commission house in 1849, the conditions were such in England that the English commission firm could only sell the cotton at a loss. They informed the New York firm who notified the Columbus planter that the cotton had sold for less than the amount advanced him by an Apalachicola commission merchant. The planter sent an additional forty bales to England to cover his debts, but the market continued to fall and the sale of the second lot still did not meet the original advance. When the Georgian refused to pay any more, the affair was taken up in a Columbus court.[7]

An occasional over-advance was bothersome but manageable. However, the tendency in a declining British market was for a large number of advances to materialize at once.[8] When this phenomenon happened an international financial crisis was set off. If the British buyer refused to pay the draft on him because it represented more money than the cotton was worth, the bill of exchange was thrown back on every person who had passed it. Consequently, each merchant was called on immediately to reimburse his creditor and so on until the bill was finally returned to the owner of the cotton. Money brokers who innocently had bought in the money market a bill generated by an over-advance on a cotton shipment were also sucked into the financial turmoil, and suddenly all businessmen were in trouble. This very condition occurred during the Panic of 1837.[9]

Any number of variables worldwide could affect the international credit structure that supported the cotton trade and clog its associated financial channels. Even when the price of cotton in Liverpool remained buoyant, nature often intervened to disrupt the even flow of cotton to market. When the water level of the river above Apalachicola suddenly fell during the period in which the residents normally relied on river transport to get their cotton to market, commission merchants were caught owing their creditors for the credit they had previously extended to the planters but without the cotton to sell to reimburse themselves. William A. Kain of Apalachicola applied to a private lender in April 1855 saying, "Owing to the present state of water in our Rivers we are very much embarrassed in our payments and we are now very much in want of a Loan."[10]

Even when the river was boatable, factors found themselves in the same financial bind when the market was declining and planters elected to withhold their cotton from sale in hopes of a rebound. Factors had extended credit during the growing season to the farmers by borrowing money from others with the intention of selling the planters' cotton in order to repay their loans. When the planters refused to sell their crops, the factors did not have the means of repaying their creditors. Commission merchants then felt the pressure of having to meet their obligations without a means of doing so.

In both 1855 and 1858 when the cotton market faltered, the editor of the *Columbus Enquirer* admonished the growers not to hold their cotton from the market because this action would mean catastrophe for their creditors.[11] He illustrated the dilemma that the factors found themselves in by quoting a merchant: " 'A, who makes 175 bales, sent me a portion of cotton when it was selling at 14 cents. Cotton commenced to decline, and, at this time, it would not bring enough to pay my acceptance on it. The draft is due to-morrow, and I must either pay the draft myself, get extensions or let the cotton be sold, making up the . . . deficit out of my own funds, and incur the displeasure of one of my best customers. I shall *sell this cotton*'" [emphasis his].[12]

Whenever cotton was withheld from the market, either because of the state of the river or by the will of the growers, the international credit structure constricted and money tightened North and South. The entire credit order was based on short-term loans that were soon in arrears when the cotton did not go forward. "Kiting" was a method by which these loans were indirectly renewed. By this method due bills were paid by drawing a second bill to pay off the first one. When misused, these bills could continue to run back and forth without ever being paid, and thus were known as "racehorse bills."[13] Nevertheless, most were not used to avoid repaying debts but were utilized by businessmen who had no access to long-term credit yet needed a means of extending their short-term loans.[14]

As an example of this form of credit extension, take the case of Austin and Long of Apalachicola who, when a hurricane badly damaged the cotton crop of 1851 just at harvest time, drew a bill at sixty days' sight on Farish Carter to meet one already due in New York.[15] The factors thus produced an extension of sixty days plus the amount of time required to transport the bill to Carter for his acceptance. Of course, eventually both loans would have to be re-paid, and with the crop destroyed or damaged, the firm ultimately suffered a loss.[16]

When advances were made with promissory notes rather than bills of exchange, the credit extension it produced was similar. The planter signed a note to his factor, who endorsed it. The planter could then discount this note at the bank. Eventually, the note would be met with the proceeds of the cotton sale.

Margaret Myers, in her study of the New York money market, concluded that the promissory note was used much more often than the bill of exchange. In fact, she considered it to be the basis of trade between the South and New York.[17] However, in the Apalachicola/ Chattahoochee River valley this was not the case. Only occasionally were cotton sales financed with promissory notes,[18] and these instances involved planters and their inland merchants only.

At Apalachicola, William G. Porter explained to a customer that the usual method of obtaining an advance there in 1855 was by drawing bills of exchange on the factors and discounting them with a bank agent.[19] D. K. Dodge of Apalachicola wrote the New York firm of Abraham Bell and Son in 1846 that he had advanced money to a planter for cotton consigned to an associated firm in Liverpool and had reimbursed himself for those advances by drawing on Bell at thirty days' sight.[20] Brown Brothers and Company, the well-known merchant-banking firm of New York, used bills of exchange to finance all the cotton purchased for them by their agent in Apalachicola.[21]

L. F. E. Dugas routinely drew drafts on his consignees in order to reimburse himself.[22] For example, when he purchased cotton for account of Messrs. Poirier Freres of New York, he notified them that he had drawn on them at sixty days' sight for $10,000 in favor of the Bank of Charleston's agency at Apalachicola.[23] The bank agency had previously lent Dugas the money with which to advance money to the grower, and the buyers repaid the bank in this way.[24]

A letter from an Apalachicola house to a New York buyer explained why bills of exchange were preferred over promissory notes there. In it the Floridians apologized for a delay in processing a purchase order because Florida money had depreciated relative to the bank notes from Georgia. "Georgia money being almost invariably required in paymt., . . . can only be had for *bills*" [his emphasis].[25] The writer continued by saying that his firm obtained Georgia money by drawing on the New York firm at sixty days' sight.

Ultimately the credit network ended in England. A few large commission houses there financed the bulk of American cotton exports. Because the South had relatively little use for the sterling bills of exchange generated by the cotton trade, most commission merchants in the Apalachicola/Chattahoochee River valley who consigned cotton to England drew their bills on the English houses' New York affiliates.

As in the other river economies of the South, Brown Brothers of New York and the associated firm of Brown, Shipley and Company of Liverpool had the largest presence as financiers in the Apalachicola/Chattahoochee River region. In the decade of the 1840s alone, at least forty-four different commission merchants in Columbus, Apalachicola, and locations in between consigned cotton to the Browns.[26] In Apalachicola the firm was represented by agent Samuel Cassin who bought cotton from local commission merchants and drew on either of the Brown houses (depending on whose account the cotton was credited) to cover his advances to them. He usually received one percent commission from the Browns for procuring the consignments. The Browns paid Cassin out of the funds they routinely charged the local factors for negotiating an advance.[27]

Because these and almost all other cotton sales were transacted on a credit basis, the cost of borrowing money was as important as the price of cotton in determining profitability. The expense of borrowing money was extremely high in this region where the amount of credit available never equaled the demand for it. Cotton factors passed along their costs to customers, while adding an additional percentage for their trouble and exposure. Those at the bottom of the credit chain bore the greatest expense. Even though annual interest rates in the tri-state area of the Apalachicola/Chattahoochee River valley were legally never higher than 8 percent,[28] planters passively accepted rates of three times that amount as the cost of doing business. For example, from August to December of 1854 Benjamin Ellison, an Apalachicola factor, advanced money to C. C. Yonge on which Ellison charged a 2.5 percent fee for making the advance plus 8 percent interest for this four-month loan. These charges meant that the annual interest rate totaled over 34 percent.[29]

In addition to receiving fees for advancing money and extending credit, southern factors also received commissions of 2.5 percent for accepting bills of exchange or endorsing the planters' promissory notes.[30] Because acceptances would be paid for by future cotton sales, the factor would have the money to pay them so long as the price of cotton remained firm. In the case of endorsements, the factor was merely lending his good name to the planter so that the latter could discount his note at the bank. The commission merchant was out no money unless the planter defaulted.

Of course, the merchant was responsible for the recompense if a planter did not honor his debt, and one never knew when he would be called on. An attorney in Columbus wrote Farish Carter during the depression following 1837 to say, "I . . . had succeeded . . . in Saving my property and what is a little more remarkable for a man living in Columbus, my credit and my character too" when along came an unexpected "security debt."[31] Similarly Nelson Tift, prominent businessman and founder of Albany, Georgia, found himself being sued by a creditor when the maker of a note that he had endorsed ran away to Texas.[32]

Because finance was such an integral part of a cotton factor's business, much of his day was consumed in performing rather involved banking activities. For instance, when selling just one man's cotton, an agent for Nourse, Brooks and Company of Apalachicola found it necessary to make three different transactions. He first had to draw on the New York house that bought it, then sell this exchange in order to procure Georgia money before he could give the grower the advance.[33]

Buying and selling exchange was a necessary sideline to the commission business. After members of J. Day and Company drew several bills on New Orleans in order to reimburse themselves for cotton sent there, they found they had more than they could dispense with and, therefore, advertised they had exchange on New Orleans for sale.[34] Their competitors Harper and Holmes found themselves in need of some way to pay a debt they had in New York and advertised that they wanted to *buy* exchange on New York "for Georgia money."[35] Thomas L. Mitchel had such a large business in exchange that he was able to offer the public "[d]rafts on New York and Providence, at sight, in sums to suit purchasers."[36] Merchants like William G. Porter were at a decided advantage over competitors when they were able to serve simultaneously as the official of a chartered bank agency.

Commission merchants even occasionally accepted deposits from customers, but like professional bankers in the South at that time, they usually did not pay interest on it. John Horry Dent routinely left a portion of his "cotton funds" with his factor E. B. Young.[37] Similarly, William Kain of Apalachicola accepted from George Hawkins a note to the latter by Farish Carter that Hawkins had been unable to negotiate at the banks. Kain wrote Carter to certify that the note had been deposited in his office subject to Carter's order.[38]

The job of cotton factor required that one be proficient at many different vocations simultaneously. Second in importance to being a shrewd buyer and seller was being a financier. Because every aspect of the cotton trade relied on credit, its availability could make or break a dealer. Without a line of credit established with a commission house in New York or Europe, a factor in Apalachicola could not buy the first bale.

The coastal factor found his station within the interconnected succession of financial transactions necessary to export cotton from the Old South. He tapped the resources of New York in order to pay the upriver cotton planter and made his living in the process. With the various commissions he charged for providing credit to his customers, there was ample opportunity for making a good living. His position between the two was precarious, however, for he was exposed from both sides. As the planter's creditor he could be ruined by another's insolvency while as debtor to the New York commission house he could be done in by circumstances beyond his control.

Because cotton was the backbone of the entire American economy its movement to market in the fall of every year put great seasonal stress on the nation's banking structure as credit tightened. For that reason, many national and international financial panics occurred in the autumn.[39] But until a national banking structure could be forged to remedy this situation, cotton merchants simply adapted to the conditions at hand, and the cotton went forth.

# 6

## *Cotton Men*

IN THE AUTUMN OF EVERY YEAR, BOTH COTTON AND cotton men converged on Apalachicola, and the local news editor heralded the coming business season.

Vessels are making their appearance in the bay, and lighters are passing and repassing laden with their omniferious freight. The ringing of the auction bell—the cries of the auctioneer—the puffing and blowing of the steamers as they traverse the waters, remind us of the busy scenes that will ensue when they come booming down the river with their tall chimneys just peeping over the bales of cotton. . . . Horses and drays are running hither and thither as if anxious to hurry along the time when they can get a load. . . . In a few weeks our wharves will be covered with cotton—our streets filled with people, and the places of business and amusement opened and every inducement held out to those who wish to enter the field of competition and struggle on for wealth. Again, and again, will the latest news be sought for; and again will the speculator rub his hands, and laugh or look sad and put them in his breaches pocket as his anticipations again are realized or blasted. . . . Onward and onward will roll the wheels of fortune.[1]

As the new season began, the cotton merchants arrived, set up their offices and dormitories in one of the forty-three brick warehouses that lined the waterfront, and prepared themselves for another busy winter. "So you want to know how we live," wrote the clerk of Goldstein and Company to his family in New York, "you've seen a horse in a mill or a squirrel in a cage—well, so we live—we have a large three story brick warehouse in the rear of the second floor of which are two rooms—one is the counting room & immediately adjoining is our sleeping room, Harry & myself. This is very convenient as we can be as late & as early at business as we please. We feed at the Hotel where we have as good a table as we ever sat down to. . . . In the evening we sit in our offices & play whist, or read papers when they come or write letters."[2]

Living so closely to his work was both an advantage and a disadvantage for young John Chrystie who came to Florida in the late 1830s. During his second business season in Apalachicola, he wrote "I hate the sight of a Cotton bale & yet the fates have ordained that some ten or fifteen thousand of them should be eternally under my nose. I almost fancy that I am a Cotton bale myself."[3]

John Chrystie's letters home describing his daily life are valuable since few other cotton merchants' personal letters have survived. Because cotton dealers spent most of every day writing business letters to their planter clients upstream and their buyers in other parts of the world, there was little time for personal letters. Chrystie described a typical business day in this way: "I have received about 800 bales of Cotton & loaded the ship Glide for NYk besides writing some 20 or 30 letters so you can see I am deep into the very vortex of business."[4]

When the river suddenly rose near the end of the season, Chrystie found himself unusually busy because farmers took advantage of what might be the last opportunity to ship their cotton. He then found he was receiving between seven and eight thousand bales a week and simultaneously loading five ships.[5]

But the river could just as suddenly fall, leaving the cotton merchants with nothing to do but to write another letter home. "I have no news to tell you—nothing under God's heaven hardly that can interest you—there is no excitement here of any kind except that of business & when there is none of that you can hardly imagine what a damned dull place it is. We sleep in our warehouse, we get up in the morning, go up to the hotel to breakfast, come down again, go up to dinner, come down again, go up to tea, come down again, & spend the evening either in playing whist or lolling about our rooms smoking, talking & so on."[6]

John Chrystie's letters home go far in dispelling the romantic image of a cotton merchant's life. Indeed, the job of cotton factor must have been among the most stressful means of making a living in antebellum America. Situated in the marketing sequence between the grower and the manufacturer, the factor often felt squeezed from either or both ends.

Although relations between cotton factors and planters were usually friendly, there were some aspects of the planter/factor association in which the interests of the two naturally conflicted. For example, when the price of cotton was low, planters were more willing to withhold their cotton from the market indefinitely while waiting for the market to rise. Their factors, on the other hand, were usually under financial pressure to sell the cotton as soon as they received it so that they could repay the loan they had made (using the planter's cotton as collateral) in order to make an advance to the planter.

In most cases when factors were caught in this sort of financial bind, they diplomatically couched their resentment toward their clients in tactful letters of entreaty. In only one instance known to the author was a valley merchant so piqued by his client's intransigence that his true feelings were evident. In that case a Marianna, Florida, merchant wrote the wealthy Georgian, Farish Carter, to compel him to decide what he wished done with the cotton being held for Carter: "I have been waiting patiently to hear from you relative to the cotton which we have had on hand for you ever since the 1st of Nov. last. . . . We do not wish to hold this cotton at our risk, and it will in a very short time be impossible to have it carried down the Chipola. . . . [W]hen [your son] was at Neal's Landing on the *Eagle* Steamer, he could without much expense or waste of time rode [*sic*] out 18 miles to attend to his business. . . . But what is a few thousand pounds of cotton to a man of millions at his disposal?"[7]

Cotton factors were once portrayed as being a monolithic entre-preneurial force whose interests fell in direct opposition to their clients.[8] However, the merchants' business fortunes were closely tied to their clients', and the planter was far from being powerless in the marketing of his crop.

Often the grower consigned his crop to a merchant with the caveat of setting a price under which the cotton could not be sold. Alexander Allen of Bainbridge made this kind of arrangement when he shipped eight bales to the coast and "limited" the price to ten cents.[9] In another instance, a planter, hoping to capitalize on a rising New York cotton market, demanded of D. K. Dodge of Apalachicola that the New York commission merchant to whom Dodge consigned the cotton not sell the staple until just before the bill of exchange drawn by Dodge on New York came due.[10]

If a planter was not satisfied with the services he received from a commission merchant he could always find another. In 1841 John Horry Dent sold his cotton to five different buyers and stored the crop in three different Eufaula warehouses. The next year he con-signed his entire crop to I. M. Wright of Apalachicola. In the 1850s Dent dealt primarily with his friend E. B. Young of Eufaula, but never exclusively.[11]

Growers who sold their crop in Columbus in 1854 found they had considerable clout when they acted concertedly. When cotton buyers collectively agreed to charge the planters for the first month of storage even if the cotton was bought "in the street" and never stored, a major brouhaha erupted. The planters' furor over this policy was so loud and immediate that the buyers soon rescinded their edict and restored their old policy.[12]

Because the planters were generally not obligated to any one factor,[13] relations between the two groups were, for the most part, cordial and trusting. As mentioned, John Horry Dent, the wealthy Alabama planter, had such a relationship with factor and commis-sion merchant E. B. Young of Eufaula. After years of doing business with each other, the two families were united when Young's daugh-ter married Dent's son.[14]

Relations among the various cotton merchants, like those be-tween factor and planter, were generally cooperative. Like any other businessmen, the valley's cotton traders attempted to capture their market share through both combinations and competition. Both Apalachicola and Columbus had chambers of commerce made up primarily of cotton merchants interested in promoting trade and settling differences among themselves.

In 1842, the Apalachicola organization sponsored a contest among upriver farmers offering silver pitchers and cups to the best and next-best lots of cotton of fifty, twenty, and ten bales submitted to them.[15] The merchants hoped the contest would encourage planters to take more care in the cultivation and preparation of their harvest in order to boost Apalachicola's reputation for quality. The businessmen were disappointed that only eleven planters entered their contest,[16] but they renewed the competition the following season, this time raising the value of the prizes.

In announcing the new contest in May 1843, president David G. Raney admitted the disappointment the businessmen had felt in the results of the first year, but again encouraged the planters to cooperate "with the Chamber in their exertions to improve the culture of this our great staple, upon which the comfort and happiness of one half the human race depends."[17]

Besides the formal activities of the Apalachicola Chamber of Commerce, the coastal factors may have combined informally to promote their interests, as Eufaula merchants accused them of doing. In 1848 and 1849 the upriver businessmen complained that Apalachicolans had formed a "combination" in setting freight rates and other charges that were unfavorable to the Alabamians.[18]

Whereas in Apalachicola cotton factors organized in order to benefit mutually, in Columbus any organization among cotton merchants was more apt to be for the sake of competition. In 1845 two rival cartels developed in the Georgia town. The owners of four "fire-proof" cotton warehouses advertised the advantages of storing cotton with them by reminding planters of their savings in fire insurance premiums, and they established their own storage rate schedule.[19]

Apparently in response to this combination, another group of warehouse owners formed a "chamber of commerce" that devised

Silver pitcher awarded to John H. Howard of Columbus for the best lot of cotton in
1843 (Croom Collection, Photo by Michael Thomason)

its own regulations for cotton handling.[20] Reacting to this organization, one of the warehouse owners of the original organization published a notice, saying, "The undersigned have reason to believe that the impression has been made on the minds of some of the Planters, that proprietors of *Fire Proof Ware Houses* are connected with this 'Chamber of Commerce,' and will try to carry into effect their rules; we unhesitatingly pronounce any such assertions *untrue, and intended to deceive*" [emphasis theirs].[21]

Another member of the "Fire Proof Ware Houses" advertised simultaneously that they too had been wrongly identified with "the Chamber of Commerce and their rules." This involvement the firm denied and vowed not to operate under the chamber's rules. "Feeling entirely willing to *live and let live*, we have not changed our rates of Storage from what has been heretofore charged" [emphasis theirs].[22]

Throughout the 1840s competition among Columbus commission merchants was keen, and they devised many different ways of getting an edge on their rivals. The firm of Ellis and Livingston advertised that it would buy plantation supplies free of charge for those who consigned their cotton to them for sale.[23] B. A Sorsby vowed to insure free all cotton stored with him.[24] Both Sorsby and the firm of Thom and Hardin promised their customers they would not speculate in cotton.[25] The latter firm's executives also offered to furnish the growers "good information on Foreign markets" as soon as they received it, and they limited their seasonal storage rate to what other warehouses charged for only the first month.[26]

Occasionally conflicts developed among the river's cotton merchants over the nonpayment of debts. In most cases the disagreements centered on the alleged failure of the defendant to honor either his promissory note or an "acceptance" (a bill of exchange after having been accepted).[27]

For the most part, however, the relations among cotton merchants were amicable, especially among factors of different cities, because the nature of the cotton business mandated close and confidential relationships. The daybook of the firm of Redd and Johnson of Columbus for the year 1852 alone illustrates how often commission merchants exchanged business. In that one year Redd and Johnson recorded accounts (both payable and receivable) for such services as storing, buying, selling, draying, and mending cotton with at least nine Columbus cotton merchants and nine Apalachicola firms.[28]

Because the cotton factorage system required that factors pass the credit burden along to the firms to whom they sold or consigned the cotton, close personal relationships among all associates were mandatory. Each acceptor of a bill of exchange drawn against a cotton shipment had to trust the person who drew it because the future of his own financial well-being lay in the hands of the people below him in the credit chain.

Whenever factors referred to the commission houses that accepted their drafts and bought or sold their cotton, whether in their correspondence or in newspaper advertisements, they always called them "friends." For example, a typical cotton firm's advertisement in the valley's newspapers was this one by William H. Kimbrough and Company of Apalachicola: "Liberal advances on cotton consigned to their friends in New York, Boston, Liverpool, or Havre."[29] This term was so universal that it undoubtedly indicated a genuine feeling of respect and trust among the associates.

Because of the necessity of relying on their associates for financial backing and confidential information, many business relationships were based on kinship. Several Apalachicola firms were headed by brothers like Jeremiah and Daniel J. Day and W. A. and P. C. Kain.[30] William H. Young, an entrepreneur of both Apalachicola and Columbus, and his brother Edward B. Young at Eufaula, Alabama, assisted one another in their cotton affairs.

The principals of several other firms were linked by marriage. For instance, the Columbus firm of Yonge and Spencer were actually father and son-in-law.[31] L. F. E. Dugas of Apalachicola and his brother-in-law in Columbus, Paul Rossignol, worked in association from opposite ends of the river, one buying cotton upriver and forwarding it to the other on the coast who sold it to overseas buyers.[32]

The aggressive and energetic go-getters established related offices in several locations within the river valley. In addition to having businesses at both ends of the Chattahoochee River, William H. Young had an agent at Albany, Georgia, at the head of the Flint River, who made advances on cotton and then forwarded it to Young's company at the coast.[33] The firm of Hill and Dawson also had branches at both Columbus and Apalachicola, and the business known as Sims and Cheever operated stores at both Albany, Georgia, and Apalachicola.[34]

Occasionally, Apalachicola firms had branch offices in other ports. Brothers Jeremiah and Daniel J. Day operated their cotton commission business from offices in Apalachicola and New York, giving them a great strategic advantage in financing and insuring their northern-bound shipments.[35] Three Apalachicola firms had branches in New Orleans, and this second location facilitated the buying of western groceries for their planter customers up the Apalachicola River as well as giving both agencies the option of selling cotton in another market when conditions were more favorable there.[36]

Even when a merchant confined his business to one site, he rarely went into business alone. Of the 101 known Apalachicola factors who marketed cotton between 1840 and 1860, 90 percent are known to have had a partner at least once in their career.[37] An even more remarkable feature of the river entrepreneurs was the informality and frequency with which they formed and dissolved partnerships.

A good illustration of this point can be made with the case of Hampton S. Smith of Columbus. In 1841 Smith formed a warehouse and commission business with Augustus Hayward under the name Smith and Hayward.[38] Two years later advertisements in the Columbus newspapers reveal that the business of Smith and Hayward was then known as Smith, Hayward, and Company, indicating the addition of one or more silent partners. That same year a separate business known as William A. Redd and Company was formed between Redd and Hampton S. Smith.[39] The following year, in 1844, Smith's partner Augustus Hayward died, and the business was reorganized as H. S. Smith and Company with the two principals being Smith and William A. Redd.[40] From that point

Smith's business was known by the same name (H. S. Smith and Company) but the silent partners changed every couple of years. Finally, in 1852, Smith decided to move his "planting interest West,"[41] whereupon two of the silent partners of Smith's firm bought him out.[42]

This confusing scenario of merchants' changing partners with the season was repeated by most of the valley's cotton dealers. Moreover, merchants did not feel compelled to remain in the same line of work or at the same location within the river valley. For example, at various times William H. Kimbrough directed his cotton commission business from the rival port of St. Joseph, Florida, as well as Apalachicola and Columbus.[43] Benjamin S. Hawley began a wholesale drug and paint business in Apalachicola while simultaneously opening a cotton warehouse upriver at Chattahoochee, Florida. Two years later Hawley was back in Apalachicola operating a cotton factorage business.[44]

Nelson Tift, the founder of Albany, Georgia, best exemplifies the casualness with which merchants of the day opened and closed their businesses. In 1838 Tift came to the Flint River to enter a co-partnership for the purpose of operating a commission business. The duo bought a steamboat and two barges and floated them to Apalachicola where they bought a stock of goods. Upon their return to Albany, they opened their business.[45] Only three months later Tift sold out his wares to other businessmen, thus establishing a pattern of opening and closing business that he continued throughout his career.

In 1840 Tift bought another stock of goods from another Albany merchant but found on comparing the invoices with the prices marked on the goods, that he had been swindled. In response Tift "gave him a severe chastisement first with my fists as I had nothing better and afterward on his coming at me with a dirk I . . . [used a stick] until he was glad to drop the dirk and be peasible [sic]."[46] The matter was thus settled.

One year later Tift again sold out his stock so that he could represent the county as state legislator, but as soon as he returned from the short legislative session, he again reopened his business.[47]

But six months later Tift recorded that he had sold his stock to others, and declared, "Thus I am out of business as a merchant."⁴⁸ At that point he intended on concentrating his energies on the cotton commission business, and he made some inquiries into finding a strong commission house in Charleston that would back him. However, a year later he traded some slaves for another stock of goods and store fixtures and reopened his store.⁴⁹ Eventually Tift closed this business and went into partnership with others in a drugstore.

Tift's erratic business career was typical of antebellum merchants who nonchalantly opened and closed their cotton concerns and seemingly changed their partners at whim. At the end of every cotton season, the newspapers carried several advertisements of "dissolutions," which generally related that the partnership had been ended "by mutual consent" or "by limitation" and urged all debtors to come forward to settle their accounts. As another cotton crop was being harvested along the river, advertisements announcing new business organizations appeared and invited their former customers to follow them to their new address.

Southern society accepted these changes in business associations among cotton merchants as a normal state of affairs even though most southerners shared at least a slight disdain for the commercial class in general, which was seen as being on a lower social rung than were men of the soil. Often merchants like Nelson Tift bought a plantation as soon as their business would allow it. In so doing they bought respectability, although neighbors never really forgot on which side a man's bread was buttered. It was probably a southerner who candidly remarked about Connecticut-born Thomas L. Mitchel, then living in Apalachicola, that he "pretends to farm some here but has more capacity as a merchant than a farmer."⁵⁰ Of course, most of Apalachicola's merchants were raised in the North where society lauded industry and wealth and therefore did not hold this prejudice against mercantile pursuits.

Apalachicola, like the other Gulf ports of New Orleans and Mobile, had a large Yankee population. One fourth of the American-born white citizens of New Orleans in 1850 had been born in the

North.[51] In Mobile just over 36 percent of those city leaders engaged in commerce were northern-born.[52] Harriet Amos, author of the Mobile study, commented that the Alabama city had more northerners among its civic leaders than anywhere else in the South "with the possible exception of New Orleans."[53]

Actually, Apalachicola may have had a much larger proportion of northerners in its merchant class than either of its Gulf neighbors.[54] Of the Apalachicola cotton merchants who owned a business between 1840 and 1860, 66 percent of those whose nativity is known were northern-born, compared to only 28 percent who were native southerners.[55]

This substantial Yankee population gave the port city a quality distinct from inland southern towns. The daughter of one of the most successful northern cotton factors commented that Apalachicola society had a "culture and refinement unusual in so small and primitive a town."[56] A native Virginian cotton merchant found in 1838 that many of the port's inhabitants "are of a character that would be consider'd a valuable acquisition to any place."[57]

On the other hand, since most of the northerners came to Florida only for the business season, then fled to their homes in the North in the summer, the population was transient. Apalachicola was practically abandoned every summer by "the itinerant population . . . leaving the city in the possession of its *inhabitants proper*" [emphasis his].[58] A cotton clerk's wife lamented the summer exodus in July of 1840 when she wrote, "most every one has left for the north, not that I regret their absence on account of their society, only it makes the town look so dull, we have one or two families still left."[59]

At the end of every business season the local newspaper announced the imminent departure of most of the business community. In 1844 alone there were twelve notices paid for by commission merchants who appointed an agent to attend to their affairs in their absence.[60] In most years, all the city officers abandoned the port in summer. The mayorship was passed down among the extant city councilmen until all of them were gone, whereupon the community did without until autumn.[61]

Those who abandoned the coast during the summer had good reasons for doing so because yellow fever and cholera were frequent visitors. Even in those summers that were relatively healthy, the humidity was oppressive, and mildew and mold soon covered everything.[62] Everyone who could afford to leave probably did so. But because the northern-born merchants were in the majority and in a better position to leave (for they had another home), their evacuation was more conspicuous than that of others.

At the end of every summer, the locals gladly welcomed the Yankees back "for the city ha[d] 'a lean and hungry look.'"[63] Nevertheless, during those long, hot months of solitude, those left behind did not hide their resentment. In the summer of 1846 as the Mexican War was brewing, a disgruntled citizen wrote the following: "While the 'winter citizens' are at the North, 'figuring round,' the 'summer boys,' who stand by 'old Apalachi' through good and through evil report, will still be 'on hand' to guard and protect her in these belligerent times. And we can tell some of those 'winter birds' who were so anxious to fly off, when they heard of the requisition made upon the Governor of Florida, for fear of being *drafted*, that if Mexico should send a fleet round here to take us, and we should fight like Croghan's little band at Sandusky . . . and should save the city, they needn't trouble themselves to return here next winter. We could get along very well without them" [emphasis his].[64]

The local editor took another potshot at the Yankees in the autumn of 1847 when he noted the opening of the business season. "The ducks are flying over daily, and at every arrival, [of] the mail boat, we are enabled to welcome back to the "Sunny South" some of the bipeds who imitate our feathered friends aforesaid, in their habit of winging their way north at the close of spring. The fowls have one advantage over the animals, however, they improve their condition at the expense of the North."[65] Resentment was a natural emotion felt toward the part-time population that skimmed off the profits in the business season and spent the off-season in health and comfort.

Northerners must have sensed this alienation at times, yet they undoubtedly realized that Apalachicola would have dried up without their seasonal appearances, and the two groups usually inter-

acted cordially. Whatever impact this northern majority certainly
must have had on the locals regarding business and social practices
cannot be determined given the paucity of extant records. However,
it is obvious that the Yankees did adopt several southern ways.

Northerners occasionally commented on the way in which southern ports were obsessed with the cotton trade. A Yankee clerk
complained, "[B]usiness! business! is all the conversation from
Monday to Saturday, If I remain so long, I shall forget that I was
born for any thing else & imagine like the people of this Country,
that it constitutes the chief end of man." Yet northerners con-
formed, and even sacrificed the Sabbath to commerce. The same
fellow commented, "How blest are the people of the North, they at
least have one day they can devote to other and higher ends."[66]

Drinking alcohol was certainly not an exclusively southern pas-
time, yet this form of leisure was probably engaged in more frequently in Apalachicola than it was by the commercial class of New
England simply because this society of men had few alternative ways
of breaking the monotony of a life consumed otherwise by business.
Furthermore, it was generally believed that drinking alcohol immu-
nized one from the fevers that circulated in this climate.

One northerner who withstood the temptation of liquor claimed,
"I do not wonder at so many young men who come out here becoming intemperate, as . . . the facilitis [*sic*] are so great for getting
liquor & the temptation is great that if one had not that moral
courage which is only to be obtained by the assistance of the Al-
mighty, most men truly become a vagabond."[67]

The keystone of white southern institutions was slavery. To some
degree how well the northern itinerants fit into southern society
hinged on this issue. In 1846 the grand jury of Franklin County (of
which Apalachicola was the county seat) made its customary rec-
ommendations including this lament: "It is to be regretted that so
few of the population of this county are allied to the soil, by the ties
of kindred and friends—few have their homesteads here, and the
soil and *our institutions* are not blended, in the affections of a majority of our population, with the association of home and its . . .
familiar endearments" [emphasis mine].[68]

Slavery may have been the litmus test by which northerners were ultimately judged. Opponents of slavery probably kept their opinions to themselves, and a few bought chattels in order to be accepted by white Apalachicola society. Thomas Leeds Mitchel of Connecticut was an Apalachicola commission merchant for over twenty years. His daughter's memoirs reveal that Mitchel did not believe in slavery. "While he employed many negroes, he owned only three, and they had come to him imploring him to buy them, as otherwise they would be sold in the open market. They were faithful, valuable servants, and became real members of our family."[69]

Because a stranger could "buy" acceptance by acquiring slaves, many did just that. The slave census of 1850 reveals that twenty Apalachicola cotton factors and auctioneers (of a total of thirty-eight in business that year) owned slaves, or approximately 53 percent.[70] Of these twenty slave owners, 60 percent were northern-born.

However, if the northerners were merely buying respectability by purchasing chattels, that does not explain why they bought so many of them. Yankees owned more than twice as many slaves on average as did the native southern cotton merchants. (The median number of slaves held by southerners was five, while northern cotton merchants, on average, held ten slaves.) Oddly, the opposite was true of the civic leaders in Mobile, where southerners owned more than twice the average number of bondsmen as were held by Yankees.[71]

Only in Apalachicola was there such a concentration of these northern visitors. The cotton merchants of Columbus, at the opposite end of the river, were overwhelmingly (87 percent) native southerners.[72] Their only northern travel amounted to yearly treks to New York to buy merchandise for their stores.

Both upstream and downstream, a businessman was considered successful if his commissions and other profits totaled ten thousand dollars annually. A wealthy man of the 1850s was said to be anyone worth one hundred thousand dollars or more. There were only a few of these in Apalachicola, although at least seven firms were believed to bring in profits of over eight thousand dollars annually.[73] Church records may provide clues as to the success rate of the commission businesses. Twenty-five percent of the commission merchants who operated in Apalachicola between 1840 and 1860 were known to be members of the Episcopal church, the religious denomination of the southern elite.[74] Many of the cotton factors in Columbus grew wealthy by their labors and eventually owned imposing mansions in town and plantations in the country.[75]

That most of the mercantile class of Apalachicola was itinerant was unfortunate for the future of the port. It was in the northerners' interest to keep down taxes and withhold their own money from internal improvements projects. Generally speaking, they were more interested in temporary gains than in the future growth of the port.[76] Robert Royal Russel wrote, "The want in so many Southern towns of a permanent mercantile class thoroughly identified with the interests of the section deprived the South of a class which, in every community, has much to do with the undertaking of new enterprises."[77]

Apalachicola could have used a permanent merchant class to fight for road and rail connections, as well as river and harbor improvements. Without these undertakings, the town could not continue to compete with the other southern cotton ports, and by 1855 the latecomer, Galveston, Texas, had replaced it as the third largest cotton port on the Gulf of Mexico.

# 7

## *The End of an Era*

HE 1840S WERE APALACHICOLA'S HEYDAY. BUT JUST AS this star was burning its brightest, it began to dim. Even though the port continued to thrive during the remainder of the antebellum period, its growth did not keep pace with that of other cotton ports. Transportation difficulties held Apalachicola back. A port's economic health naturally depended on the ease with which products could be moved in and out, and every port had handicaps to overcome in this respect. But while the other ports were successful in remedying their shortcomings and enhancing their natural advantages, Apalachicola was not.

Navigational obstructions in the rivers and harbors of America had to be cleared before a local trade developed. After basic problems were surmounted and commerce was established, businessmen began to dream of expanding their trading region by internal improvements such as road, canal, and railroad construction that would augment the existing river travel.

The American boom in canal building began with the completion of the Erie Canal in 1825. By 1840, some three thousand miles of canals had been completed in this country.[1] Most canal projects were intended to extend river transportation by cutting around waterfalls or other obstructions to join stretches of the same river or by connecting separate river systems. Like their counterparts else-where, the Apalachicola River residents caught canal fever as well. But unlike most projects, canals there were envisioned, not as a means of extending river travel, but as a way of avoiding the shal-lows of Apalachicola Bay.[2]

Apalachicola Bay (or St. George Sound) was the only natural harbor associated with a major interior river system on the Gulf of Mexico between Pensacola and Tampa Bay. However, like most unimproved harbors, it was in need of deepening in places to attract the largest of the oceangoing vessels. Ships drawing sixteen or more feet of water could get no closer than ten miles of the city wharf, and those vessels drawing more than twelve feet could get no closer than three miles.[3] Shallow-draft boats had to lighter cargo between the oceangoers and the city docks, adding to the cost of doing business in Apalachicola.

Fortunately for the port city, none of the proposed canal projects intended to connect the river upstream with other harbors to the west was ever built. They, like thousands of other internal improve-ment projects throughout the country, succumbed to the depression following 1837. A railroad was constructed to siphon the river trade away to the rival port of St. Joseph, but after a yellow fever epidemic wiped out the upstart's populace in 1841, Apalachicola was left in control of the river trade. Businessmen there learned to cope with less-than-optimum navigational conditions in the bay and river. In the harbor, lightering cargo to the ships became second nature, and upstream people found steamboats to be remarkably adaptable to the idiosyncrasies of each river.

According to one reckoning, over one hundred commercial wa-tercraft operated on this river system between 1840 and 1860.[4] These vessels adapted their girth to the dimensions of the river. Their average size was between one hundred and two hundred tons. Most could carry their own weight in cargo while only drawing two and a half feet of water when fully loaded.[5]

The Flint and Chipola rivers, being smaller tributaries than the main stream, required even smaller boats. During the cotton season, light draft barges or "boxes" were regularly poled between Albany and Apalachicola. The Albany commission merchants who owned one line claimed that their vessels had the capacity of holding 1,500 bales "on any stage of the river, if necessary."[6] One of the largest of these barges, the *Rebecca*, measured one hundred and three feet long, over seventeen feet wide, and three feet deep. It drew only two feet when heavily loaded.[7] Cotton boxes transported cotton along the upper Chattahoochee above Eufaula, as well.[8]

However, river travel still had its drawbacks. Like most southern rivers, the Apalachicola River system was usually not boatable in the dry summer months. Fortunately for all involved in cotton marketing, the river's best boating conditions usually coincided with the cotton harvesting season. Farmers began picking cotton in September. By Christmas the river was usually high enough to allow the boats passage until late spring when the water again receded. Any cotton not in warehouse or market by that time had to wait for next season.

Of course during a few years of unusually low rainfall there was sufficient water for navigation for only a few months of the year. Once during the boating season the river level fell out so swiftly that boats were left stranded where they lay.[9] At other times, as in 1844, navigation was temporarily halted because the water level was too high to permit the boats to go under the bridges.[10] When navigation was halted, for whatever reason, towns upriver experienced shortages of salt and other necessaries while the supplies piled up in Apalachicola warehouses.[11]

Even when river conditions were optimum, steamboat travel was often dangerous. Boats carrying a full load of cotton were floating time bombs. Cotton was a highly combustible commodity. Sparks from the vessel's smokestack ignited instantaneously when they alighted on bales stored on deck. On a trip from Columbus to Apalachicola, the steamer *Franklin* loaded with 1,100 bales caught fire and all was lost.[12] Instances such as this were a common calamity. Less often, explosions occurred when the water level within the crude steam boilers became too low, creating too much pressure. The steamer *Emily* exploded shortly after leaving the Apalachicola dock in 1849, and seven people died.[13] Ten people were killed when the *Siren* exploded in 1845.[14]

The most common river accident occurred when a vessel struck a hidden obstruction that punctured the bottom of the boat. The *Retrieve* struck a rock in the Chattahoochee and sank with over one thousand bales aboard in 1853.[15] In one month in 1848 three boats were wrecked on snags.[16]

Insurance rates reflected the river's hazards, and they were higher on cotton shipped down the Apalachicola/Chattahoochee River system than on the other Gulf of Mexico tributaries. The standard insurance rate on freight from Apalachicola upriver in 1840 was 3 percent. The rate of the return trip was 2.5 percent. That same year, rates on the Alabama River system, which flowed into Mobile Bay, were only 1 percent or less. Rates for the Mississippi averaged less than 1.5 percent. Ten years later, insurance rates of the three river systems reflected the same ratios.[17]

Even with all these disadvantages, river travel was much more preferable than traveling by stage or wagon along the few roads that existed. If one wished to travel overland from Apalachicola, one had the choice of only two roads. The first led from the town on the west side of the river westward to St. Joseph, then curved northward to run along the west bank of the Chipola River to Marianna, Florida. To use the more direct road leading from the coast to the north, one had to find transportation across the wide Apalachicola estuary to East Point. This road crossed the main east-west highway (the Pensacola and St. Augustine road) just south of the Georgia border at the town of Chattahoochee.[18]

Early thoroughfares "were little more than wide paths cut through the forest."[19] In the rainy season the roads were impassable. Travelers found the Federal Road between Montgomery and Columbus, Georgia, "so rough that it was more pleasant to walk than to ride, wherever the road was dry enough to walk."[20] As late as 1854 a warning to travelers was published in the Columbus newspaper that the foundation of the main road near Lumpkin had eroded causing a thirty-foot precipice overlain with only a few feet of soft clay.[21]

Railroads had many advantages over water travel. Generally rail travel was faster and more reliable. Most steamboats seldom traveled faster than fifteen miles an hour, while trains by the 1850s maintained speeds of twenty to thirty miles an hour.[22] Additionally, trains could travel on a schedule that did not regard the seasonal level of the river and, therefore, were more dependable. Most people thought these advantages offset the substantially higher freight rates that rail lines charged. It was only a matter of time before the railroads would compete with the steamboats and win.

Charleston, South Carolina, was the first southern port city to sponsor a railroad. For many years Charleston had been suffering from a decline in income caused by the diminishing productivity of the old fields of its hinterland while the cotton farmers constantly abandoned them for new land to the west. As soon as news of the successful operation of railroads in England reached Charleston, the city, the state, and the local citizenry pooled their resources and built the first southern railroad from Charleston to near Augusta, Georgia, in 1833.

Augusta lay at the head of navigation of the Savannah River, and its trade with neighboring farmers made it the preeminent inland Georgia market in the 1830s.[23] Nearby farmers brought in their cotton by wagon and bought their supplies there. By building a railroad from Charleston, the South Carolinians diverted Augusta's cotton trade to Charleston instead of by water to Savannah.

Savannah businessmen became alarmed and in self-defense built a railroad to tap the next river system to the west whose inland market town was Macon in central Georgia.[24] (Macon lay at the head of navigation of the Ocmulgee River whose seaport was Darien, Georgia, to the south of Savannah.) The road was completed to Macon in 1843, and eventually this Central of Georgia line connected with Georgia's state-owned railroad network that stretched across northern Georgia to Chattanooga, Tennessee.

After this extension of rail lines into the upper reaches of the Mississippi and Alabama river systems, the businessmen of the preeminent Gulf of Mexico ports of New Orleans and Mobile suddenly noticed their cotton receipts diminishing. In response entrepreneurs in these gulf ports began their own railroad projects to connect them with other river systems.[25]

Columbus, Georgia, initially welcomed a railroad project that

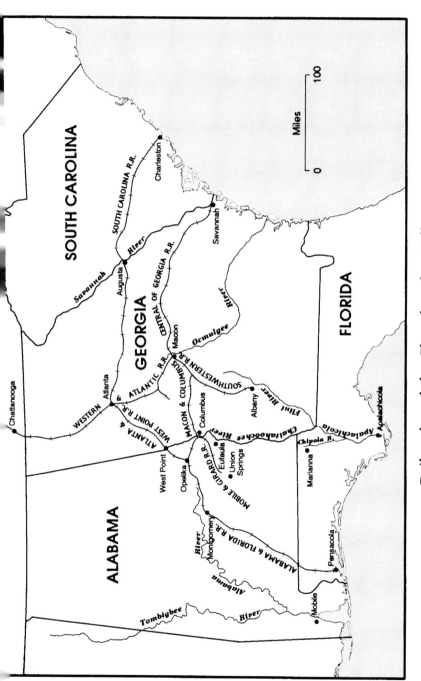

Railroads and the Chattahoochee Valley

would have connected it with the road between Savannah and Chattanooga, but the depression following 1837 snuffed out its promise.[26] However, in the 1840s steamboat travel on the Chattahoochee/Apalachicola increased phenomenally with the advent of an improved shallow-draft hull design. Columbus, at the head of navigation, became a bustling trade center where farmers from as far away as about thirty miles wagoned in their cotton and bought their supplies, and it eclipsed Augusta as the state's premier inland trading town.

Therefore, when a new wave of railroad construction washed over Georgia after 1845, Columbus met it with a "noticeable lack of enthusiasm."[27] Columbusites feared they would lose their wagon trade if the railroad extended from Savannah to them. All the cotton to the east that now was hauled by wagon into Columbus could move directly to the railroad and thence to Savannah, cutting off Columbus. Many thought of the railroad as an "iron boa" that would "eat up the wagon trade, and break down the business of the town."[28] The people took heed of the diminishing trade that Augusta and Macon witnessed after rail connection with Charleston and Savannah.[29] Indecision gripped Columbus. "In every direction around us we perceive the utmost urgency and activity in the prosecution of public improvements, designed to divert trade from its natural channel—from Columbus—and to secure it for other points,"[30] wrote a Columbus editor in 1845.

But if the railroad were to join the Chattahoochee River at another location, Columbus would be bypassed altogether. The Columbus *Times* warned its readers that if the road from Macon did not come to Columbus, Eufaula to its south might replace it as the premier market town on the Chattahoochee: "Either Eufaula or Macon becomes the grocery mart and depot, and the commerce that should have added thrift and wealth to this city, will be borne by us, through *Pond Town* on the wings of steam; and every pull of the Locomotive will remind Columbus of her folly, and echo the laugh of our sister city of Macon, at our simple-minded gullibility" [emphasis theirs].[31]

Reluctantly Columbus businessmen realized they would have to build the railroad to their city to prevent its being built elsewhere. Indeed, Milton Sydney Heath wrote that this road "may hold the unique distinction of being the only railroad ever to have been located with a view to avoiding traffic."[32]

Once the citizens had determined to connect Columbus by rail with Savannah via Macon, they worked ardently on concomitant projects which they hoped would ensure that they retain the vital wagon trade. A project to improve the Chattahoochee above the city, where several falls were located, was promoted but never acted on.[33]

Another strategy for preserving Columbus's trade surfaced around 1850. For several years there was much talk of building "plank roads" that would radiate from Columbus and make it relatively easy for outlying farmers to cart their produce into town. The idea was to make a hard-surface thoroughfare so superior to current trails that a farmer could haul in more cotton in less time.[34] Proponents believed this low-cost substitute for railroads combined with cheap steamboat transportation could successfully challenge the rails "and thus preserve the river traffic and the wagon trade."[35]

The Columbus *Times* was an eager proponent of this movement and often admonished its readers to save themselves while there was still time: "Two or three plank roads of from 25 to 40 miles length are of prime necessity to this city—indispensable to secure its legitimate trade & to *retain* some that it has—yet who moves in it? who cares? who takes the time to look beyond the doors of his counting room, to inquire how the general weal of the community of which he is part, is faring? No where else is the maxim so practically exemplified as in Columbus, that 'what's everybody's business is nobody's business'" [emphasis theirs].[36]

Plank road fever simultaneously infected other towns similarly situated at the head of navigation of their respective rivers. Albany, Georgia, on the Flint River, was "determined to have a Plank Road outlet in some direction" and promoted several routes.[37] Montgomery, Alabama, at the head of navigation of the Alabama River system worked on similar projects.[38]

Eufaula, Alabama, below Columbus, completed a plank road

from the bridge over the Chattahoochee up to the town center. The local newspaper acknowledged its completion, saying, "we can now assure our friends in Georgia, that they need no longer fear encountering a muddy, boggy hill, in bringing their cotton and other produce into our markets."[39]

Twenty-four other plank road companies were chartered in Alabama and at least another twenty-one plank road companies were chartered by the state of Georgia from 1850 to 1854.[40] Most were failures since capital was lured away by the railroads and the plank road movement "succumbed quickly to the competition of the 'iron horse.'"[41]

Savannah was the driving force behind the Georgia railroad movement. With its location on the Atlantic Ocean it could offer a more direct route to market for west Georgia cotton than via the Chattahoochee or Flint to Apalachicola, thence all the way around the Florida peninsula to its ultimate destination. Savannah's city corporation sponsored the Central of Georgia line, which joined the state-owned Western and Atlantic road at Macon in 1843. From there Savannah wanted badly to tap the rich cotton lands lying between the Flint and Chattahoochee rivers. For that purpose the city of Savannah in conjunction with the Central of Georgia company organized the Southwestern Railroad, which intended to build two lines into southwest Georgia. One line from Macon would extend westward to Columbus on the Chattahoochee. In association with this project the city of Columbus sponsored the Muscogee Railroad Company in 1845, which was simultaneously to build eastward from Columbus to join the Southwestern line. The other Southwestern line would extend southward from Macon to Albany on the Flint River.

The roads connecting Columbus to Savannah did not meet until 1853. Ironically, a riverboat from Apalachicola brought up the last of the iron spikes to complete the rail line.[42] On that day the economic structure of the Apalachicola/Chattahoochee River system was forever altered. To celebrate the completion of the line, a jubilee was held. A special train brought a group of Savannah citizens from their port on the Atlantic to Columbus for the celebration.

One speechmaker pointed out the incredible feat that had that day been accomplished: "Sober minded men, who have been used to traveling thirty-five or forty miles a day, and who have not yet realized the fearful speed of this fast generation, will scarcely believe that our friends from Savannah were whizzed along by the iron horse, a distance of three hundred miles between the rising and setting sun."[43]

Another speaker emphasized the significance of the day when he said, "[Today] is the day that unites the waters of the Gulf with the great Atlantic. It is the day which unites the commercial relations of Columbus with those of Savannah. It is the day that binds those cities together with iron bands; and we trust they are not stronger than the silken cords of kindness and feeling, which are wound around our hearts."[44] At the end of the ceremony the mayor of Columbus symbolically mixed a vial of water from the Chattahoochee River with one from the Atlantic Ocean.

The advent of the railroad disrupted the southern economic order and set formerly amicable communities in competition with each other in order to retain their market share of the cotton trade. Fierce trade rivalries developed among port cities. Farther inland, towns situated on different river systems conspired to steal each other's trade.

The Columbus *Times* editor warned the public in 1848 not to sleep over their interests. "We are surrounded by enterprising, active, go-ahead rivals, and we shall have to struggle for the prize of prosperity and advancement, if not of existence, if we hope to win it from the *Athletoe* who are our competitors" [emphasis his].[45] Any observant reader of the local newspapers should have shared his opinion.

Even before the railroad was completed to Columbus, Savannah merchants had begun advertising in the Columbus newspapers. Furthermore, the commercial columns of these newspapers began routinely running the cotton market reports of Savannah, Augusta, Charleston, Montgomery, and Mobile, while reports from Apalachicola appeared less and less frequently.[46]

Inland trading towns that once had had little competition among themselves because they were located on different transportation routes now found the rules of commerce had changed. Macon on the Ocmulgee River competed with Columbus and Albany. Montgomery on the Alabama River system contended with Columbus and Macon. Albany fought back by urging the improvement of the Flint River to keep open its Gulf of Mexico outlet while courting the Southwestern Railroad, which eventually extended its road to this Flint River port in 1857.[47]

Even more curious was the competition for trade that emerged among the communities of the same river system. Fort Gaines, Georgia, on the Chattahoochee River outflanked Eufaula to its north by securing a rail connection in 1854.[48] After Columbus was connected with the railroad to Savannah in 1853, it jealously guarded this advantage from Eufaula to the south. The *Times and Sentinel* warned its readers that it was vital to their interests that Eufaula not have direct rail connections to Savannah: "By our connections with the Atlantic, we command the trade of an immense region west of us but let a road be built from Union Springs to Savannah via Eufaula, and our prosperity would melt like the mists of the morning."[49]

Eufaula made early overtures to Columbus to link the two cities by rail, as well as by water, but Columbus realized Eufaula could siphon off some of its cotton trade in this way. Eufaula then set its sights on securing a more direct connection with the Atlantic. When it was finally successful in gaining the promise of an extension of the Southwestern Railroad to it, Columbusites suddenly became very generous toward their southern neighbors.

The supercilious sneers made before the former secured a commitment from the Southwestern Railroad[50] evolved into magnanimous gestures of goodwill after Columbus's superiority was challenged. Now the Columbus editor addressed Eufaula, invoking fear of their common foes, and solicited Eufaula to build a railroad from there to Columbus, which indirectly linked Eufaula to the Atlantic. The editor of the *Enquirer* now cajoled: "We believe that it is some evil and mistaken jealousy of this kind which has heretofore prevented the co-operation of our own city and Eufaula in the construction of a railroad connecting the two, and which has now turned the attention of the latter to a connection with the Southwestern Railroad at Cuthbert."[51] The writer went on to list the numerous reasons why Eufaula's interest would be better served if it built a railroad to Columbus rather than via the Southwestern line.

Columbus had been slow to realize the consequences of inaction, but once it shook off its lethargy it worked faithfully, if somewhat fitfully, to retain its position as a major inland market. After the line to Macon was completed, city leaders hungrily turned their sights on the vast cotton lands of southern Alabama. In May 1853, the same month the tracks were completed to Savannah, Columbus leaders approached Mobile about a joint railroad project between their cities. This would give Columbus the advantage of having rail connections to both the Gulf of Mexico and the Atlantic Ocean, and city leaders hoped the plan would also thwart the construction of a rival road being planned to extend from Montgomery to Mobile. Montgomery had already completed a rail line to the Chattahoochee River thirty miles above Columbus at West Point, so the planned road from Montgomery to Mobile would bypass Columbus on its extension from the Gulf to Atlanta, Georgia, where several rail lines converged.[52]

Mobilians favored the line to Columbus because they had recently become competitors of Montgomery, their former trading partner upstream. Montgomery merchants had established direct steamboat communication between themselves and New Orleans that had bypassed Mobile. Therefore, Mobilians overwhelmingly supported the railroad known as the Mobile and Girard line to Columbus.[53]

Unfortunately for Mobile and Columbus, they were slow to raise the money for the project, and in the meantime, Montgomery built a rival line to Pensacola, Florida, on the Gulf Coast. In 1855 the Montgomery line had also completed a spur line to Columbus from Opelika, Alabama. Thus Columbus was connected by rail to Montgomery and Pensacola, and Montgomery superseded Columbus as the marketing center for the cotton of southeastern Alabama.[54]

The Mobile and Girard line was completed only to Union Springs, Alabama, by 1860, a distance from Columbus of only about fifty miles. This line did not necessarily hurt Columbus, though, because this short road was used almost exclusively for hauling cotton *into* Columbus. If the line had been completed to Mobile before the war, farmers along this road could have opted to send their cotton southward to market at the Alabama port, thus cutting Columbus off from some of this trade. However, receipts in Columbus from the Mobile and Girard road dramatically rose as the construction progressed. Four to five hundred bales per day came in over this line in October 1858, and the company had to add an extra freight train to pick up seven hundred and fifty bales in excess that accumulated along the Alabama line.[55] Alabama growers dispatched to Columbus almost thirteen thousand bales during only two months that fall.[56]

The advent of the railroad into the Chattahoochee River valley clearly affected the course of the cotton trade. By securing a rail linkage, Columbus ensured its future prosperity. Table 7-1 is a compilation of the cotton receipts for the years 1840 through 1861. Columbus receipts generally increased in those two decades, culminating in 1859 when the city received almost 112,000 bales. There were only two periods when receipts decreased. During the years 1849 through 1852 the Columbus market shrank, probably because of the approach of the railroad from the east, which allowed farmers east of Columbus to cart their cotton directly to the railroad instead of bringing it west to the Chattahoochee. In the years 1857 and 1858 the receipts again receded, but this drop was likely because of bad harvests. All the American cotton ports except Galveston, Texas, witnessed a decrease in their 1858 returns as compared to the year before.[57]

Apalachicola's fate was not so fair. As can be seen from Table 7-2, cotton receipts there during the 1840s moved generally upward as did the valley's total production. Figures are unavailable for the crop of 1854, the first season the railroad operated. However, in 1855 Apalachicola receipts showed a dramatic decline compared to the returns prior to the advent of the railroad. The difference between

**Table 7-1.** Columbus Cotton Receipts, 1840–1861*

| Year | Bales Received |
|------|---------------|
| 1840 | 52,700 |
| 1841 | 36,192 |
| 1842 | 40,993 |
| 1843 | 58,095 |
| 1844 | 62,331 |
| 1845 | 82,466 |
| 1846 | 49,003 |
| 1847 | 55,797 |
| 1848 | 56,796 |
| 1849 | 67,300 |
| 1850 | 59,519 |
| 1851 | 55,059 |
| 1852 | 42,976 |
| 1853 | 65,020 |
| 1854 | 71,530 |
| 1855 | 65,379 |
| 1856 | 100,628 |
| 1857 | 80,245 |
| 1858 | 75,670 |
| 1859 | 111,931 |
| 1860 | Unknown |
| 1861 | 83,166 |

*These statistics were compiled from the following sources: 1840–47, Columbus *Times*, 4 January 1848; 1848, ibid., 13 June 1848, p. 3; 1849, *Columbus Enquirer*, 4 September 1849; 1850, Martin, *Columbus, Geo.*, II: 43; 1851, *Columbus Enquirer*, 24 June 1851, p. 3; 1852, ibid., 18 May 1852, p. 3; 1853, ibid., 10 July 1855, p. 3; 1854, Columbus *Times and Sentinel*, 18 July 1854, p. 3; 1855–56, *Columbus Enquirer*, 9 September 1856, p. 3; 1857, Hinton, "Trade and Transportation at Columbus, Ga.," p. 25; 1858–59, *Columbus Enquirer*, 20 April 1859, p. 3; 1861, Hinton, "Trade and Transportation at Columbus, Ga.," 25.

**Table 7-2.** Apalachicola Cotton Receipts, 1840–1860*

| Year | Bales Received |
| --- | --- |
| 1840 | 52,583 |
| 1841 | 61,549 |
| 1842 | 86,864 |
| 1843 | 125,340 |
| 1844 | 105,934 |
| 1845 | 151,609 |
| 1846 | 110,902 |
| 1847 | 109,461 |
| 1848 | 119,880 |
| 1849 | 143,223 |
| 1850 | 130,240 |
| 1851 | 135,142 |
| 1852 | 139,937 |
| 1853 | 139,604 |
| 1854 | Unknown |
| 1855 | 83,321 |
| 1856 | 96,725 |
| 1857 | 80,361 |
| 1858 | 67,941 |
| 1859 | 108,382 |
| 1860 | 133,079 |

*These statistics were compiled from the following sources: 1840, Apalachicola *Gazette*, 4 April 1840, quoted in Lovett, "Excerpts and Articles"; 1841, *Florida Journal*, 1 May 1841, quoted in Lovett, "Excerpts and Articles"; 1842, Carter, *Territorial Papers of the United States*, 26: 587; 1843, *Commercial Advertiser*, 8 January 1844, p. 2; 1844, the total receipts in this year were derived by adding the weekly receipts listed in the Apalachicola *Commercial Advertiser*, 1 January 1844–30 June 1844; 1845, ibid., 17 July 1846, p. 3; 1846–47, ibid., 6 October 1847, p. 2; 1848, ibid., 22 July 1848, p. 3; 1849, *Commercial Advertiser Prices Current*, 21 April 1851, p. 1; 1850, Owens, "Apalachicola Before 1861," p. 221; 1851, *Mobile Register*, 26 June 1851, p. 2; 1852–53, *Commercial Advertiser Prices Current*, 9 May 1853; 1855–57, *Columbus Enquirer*, 8 September 1857, p. 3; 1858–59, *Mobile Register*, 30 June 1859, p. 3; 1860, *Florida House Journal*, 1860, p. 15.

the 1853 and 1855 receipts amounted to approximately a 41 percent drop. Although up slightly the next year, Florida receipts continued their downward trend through the poor cotton season of 1858. In the last two years before the Civil War cotton sent to Apalachicola increased again, but so did those of every market. The introduction of the railroad into the interior had encouraged planters to open new fields. There was simply more cotton produced in the late 1850s than ever before, but Apalachicola's share of this production was dwindling.

Using the 1850 and 1860 agricultural censuses of every county in the Apalachicola/Chattahoochee River valley, Harry P. Owens derived the most telling statistics of how Apalachicola was affected by the railroad incursion. In 1850, farmers in the river basin harvested 163,973 bales of cotton. Ten years later the same area produced 303,841 bales, for an increase of 54 percent.[58] However, this rise in receipts actually reflected a decrease in Apalachicola's share of the valley's total crop, from just over 79 percent in 1850 to slightly more than 43 percent a decade later.[59] Therefore, while the valley's cotton production had doubled, Apalachicola's share of the market had been slashed almost in half.

Nature also contributed to the downturn in Apalachicola receipts after the railroad entered the valley. One month before the line between Columbus and Savannah was completed, the Savannah *Courier* prophetically stated, "If the next fall should be a dry one, this road will bring to Savannah, during the next year, fifty thousand bales of Cotton, which have heretofore gone to the Gulf ports."[60] Rainfall was so low during the 1854–55 season that the river did not allow steamboat traffic until late March 1855.[61] By that time most of the cotton had been shipped by rail. As if to add insult to injury, the lack of river flow caused the Apalachicola Bay to silt up. The largest of the oceangoing vessels now had difficulty entering St. George Sound.

The railroads in and out of Columbus were immediately successful. Early in the season after the completion of the railroad, a Savannah newspaper glowingly reported that the Atlantic port had received 3,000 bales directly from Columbus in one week, "which,

**Table 7-3.** Savannah Cotton Receipts, 1842–1859*

| Year | Bales Received |
|------|----------------|
| 1842 | 299,173 |
| 1843 | 243,304 |
| 1844 | 305,016 |
| 1845 | 189,076 |
| 1846 | 236,029 |
| 1847 | 245,496 |
| 1848 | 406,906 |
| 1849 | 340,025 |
| 1850 | 312,294 |
| 1851 | 351,566 |
| 1852 | 353,068 |
| 1853 | 315,521 |
| 1854 | 388,366 |
| 1855 | 395,866 |
| 1856 | 328,836 |
| 1857 | 294,518 |
| 1858 | 470,445 |
| 1859 | 536,008 |

*These figures are tabulated in *DeBow's Review*, 15 (July 1853): 105–06, and 29 (November 1860): 670.

if it were not for railroad facilities and low freights might, as in former years, have found their way to Apalachicola."[62]

One month later a Columbus businessman wrote his brother, saying, "The river here is navigable, but boats doing very little. Most of the cotton, goes off now to Savannah direct, by the Rail Road."[63]

Three years later the *Columbus Enquirer* remarked that the river that autumn was probably too low for the larger steamers to get through, but added: "Very little cotton, however, will be shipped from this city this winter by the river, unless the railroads should be unable to keep up with the demand for shipment."[64]

Apalachicola had seen this trouble coming. Back in 1846 the Franklin County Grand Jury remarked, "It is certainly a matter of wonder and remark that a city exporting over one hundred and fifty thousand bales of Cotton . . . has no avenue of ingress except by water. The wilderness and the swamps, imperious and impenetrable surround us."[65]

Two years later in 1848 an Apalachicola citizen warned his neighbors that the railroad then moving west toward the Flint and Chattahoochee rivers would soon do them in: "It is obvious that this town will soon be well nigh annihilated, unless we take means to avert, as far as lies in our power, impending ruin. I allude to the rail roads of Georgia. . . . [T]he circle of trade, that *once* centered at Columbus, Geo., has been circumscribed by the influence of the Macon and Western rail road: increase of production in the circumscribed circle has blinded our eyes to the true state of the case" [emphasis his].[66]

That same year another Apalachicola writer cautioned, "That the success of our neighbors in carrying out their projects must inflict a serious blow on the commerce of this city no one denies."[67] This person urged the community to do something "to obviate" the consequences of the proposed Muscogee road [from Columbus to Savannah]."[68] For several years thereafter the Floridians talked of building a plank road to Gadsden County, Florida, a prolific farming area with limited access to the Apalachicola River.[69] The proposed road would have broadened Apalachicola's existing market by augmenting the river trade. Yet nothing was done.

Most other proposals for saving Apalachicola's livelihood called for improvement of the Flint River trade. There was brief talk of building a plank road that would parallel that river between Bainbridge and Albany,[70] but most of the attention centered on improving river transportation. One plan called for dredging the river channel to (and even above) Albany so that Macon's rail connection could not draw off the cotton of southwestern Georgia.

A second scheme involved building boats more suitable to the shallow, twisting river.[71] Both plans hoped to achieve regular communication between southwestern Georgia and the Gulf of Mexico. Even after Albany had rail connections, the local newspaper editor claimed that if freighting was reasonable and regular by water, the town would certainly prefer it to the train.[72]

Words spoke louder than actions in Apalachicola, however. In this age when internal improvements were generally thought to be the responsibility of private citizens, they seemed unwilling to put their money where their mouths were. Instead, they seemed content to do little more than reason with the upriver farmers that it was more economical for Georgians to send their cotton to Florida than to Savannah. In 1849 and 1854 anonymous writers for the Albany *Patriot* went to great lengths to explain to planters how much cheaper it was to use water transportation to Apalachicola than it was to wagon their harvest to the railroad at Macon.[73]

It is curious that Apalachicolans were so inactive when it came to their livelihood. Perhaps this inertia was because of the transient nature of most of the business community who lived there only during the cotton marketing season. These men were accustomed to thinking in the short term. They commonly moved their addresses with the season, and it was easier for them to move to other markets than to reach into their pockets to pay for modernizing the languid port. At least one Apalachicola factor moved to Savannah as soon as the railroad to Columbus was completed.[74]

Apalachicola businessmen attempted only two private enterprises that would have made Apalachicola more appealing as a marketing center. One group built a steamer of light enough draft to run between Columbus and the bay during the summer months, and another established a regular steam route between New Orleans and Apalachicola.[75] The only assertive public step the Apalachicolans took was to petition the state legislature to use Franklin County tax money to finance the dredging of the channel in Apalachicola Bay, which by 1860 held only six and one-half feet of water at high tide.[76] Their complaints that Apalachicola had been "most grossly and shamefully neglected" by the state's internal improvement projects went unheeded in the state capitol.

By that time Apalachicola merchants seem to have been lulled by rising cotton receipts into believing the port's prosperity was re-turning. In 1860 cotton again crowded Apalachicola's wharves, and some there believed "that the natural course of trade cannot be diverted from a place like ours."[77] This smug logic continued: "The trade and commerce of the Chattahoochee and Flint rivers, are naturally tributary to us, and no matter what amount of business may be diverted from us for a time by artificial channels, in the shape of Railroads, . . . still the trade will find its way back to the old channel as sure as water will seek its own level."[78]

Some fraction of the trade that had gone to the railroads and Savannah immediately after the line was finished to Columbus may have begun to return to Apalachicola. In 1857 the Savannah factors unilaterally raised their commission rates from fifty cents per bale to 2.5 percent of the gross sale. With cotton prices up to around ten cents, this rate paid them about $1.25 per bale.[79] Farmers in the vicinity of Albany and Columbus threatened the Savannah merchants that they would not stand for this increase, and it appears they made good their threats because receipts at Savannah were lower in that year than at any other year in the 1850s.[80]

This same year Columbus merchants began noticing that railroad freight charges discriminated against them. It now seemed the generosity that Savannah had shown in paying for much of the road between the two cities, was, in reality, only self-interest. The Central of Georgia line charged little for cotton to be transported to Savannah from Columbus. In fact, businessmen from the latter city suspected cotton was carried to the Savannah market at below cost. This bargain rate of course, had the effect of drawing cotton to the Atlantic port for sale instead of to the interior market.[81] Simultaneously, the Columbus merchants noticed that the freight rates were exorbitant on their merchandise that came by rail from the North through Savannah. It appeared the railroad was compensating for loss of revenue in shipping cotton by charging extra on "up freight."[82] Because of these high freight charges, groceries and other wares cost more in Columbus than in Savannah. Interior farmers then had another inducement to trade in Savannah.

On the eve of the Civil War, which would further disrupt the river trade, the old economic order that had focused on the river was strikingly modified. Columbus then looked east and west when once it had only looked south. The location of railroads, not rivers, dictated commercial superiority.

One of the major changes in the Apalachicola/Chattahoochee River valley after the railroads penetrated it was the reversal in the direction of trade above the Florida boundary. "What was deemed improbable and visionary by many a few years since"[83] had come to pass. The Chattahoochee and Flint rivers now [ran] up stream."[84]

Both Columbus and Albany at the head of navigation of these streams now courted the business of the cotton growers south of them.[85] In 1855 a Columbus attorney commented that the river was then in good boating order, but that had done little "toward relieving our warehouses of the immense quantity of Cotton in store—for the Boats bring up about as much as they carry down."[86]

This change in trade patterns created new avenues for commerce. It now became rather commonplace to read of Sea Island cotton being boated northward form Apalachicola to Albany for rail shipment to the Savannah market, [87] or even of cotton being sent by rail from Montgomery or Macon to Columbus and then loaded onboard a steamer for Apalachicola.[88] Planters now had numerous alternatives in choosing a market for their cotton.

These options caused further alterations in the old marketing system. The former relationship between the planter and his factor became less vital. Now that the railroads came very near many farms, the grower could sell his crop at home without paying transportation costs to some distant market or commissions for forwarding and selling.[89] Telegraphic lines strung across the region in the railroads' rights-of-way enabled farmers and merchants alike to keep abreast of the latest price quotations and the going rates of freight and insurance in various markets. Faster communications meant business decisions could now be based on facts, rather than rumor.

Another change wrought by the advent of the railroads was an elongation of the marketing season. When the growers no longer had to wait for Christmas for the rivers to rise, they could send their harvest to market as they baled it. The commercial season began sooner and ended later since it no longer had any relationship to the amount of rainfall. All through the summer of 1854, cotton continued to dribble in to Columbus.[90] Cotton marketers now had some business to attend year-round, and the market was not so glutted at certain periods as it had been in the old age when the rivers first rose.

Because of the railroads, more lands were opened to cotton cultivation, and the production of the staple increased dramatically.[91] Furthermore, because the faster, more direct, and more reliable new transportation extended the geographic range of each trading center, it increased competition among distant producers and "encouraged and even demanded" greater specialization in cotton.[92] The rails further spurred a reliance on cotton by the importation of food and fertilizer from outside the region.[93]

U. B. Phillips has written that this increase in cotton production and specialization had the deleterious effect on the South of extending and intensifying the plantation system at a time when the region really needed crop diversification and economic self-sufficiency.[94] Whereas northern railroads contributed to the strength of the regional economy by encouraging industry and trade with the West, southerners viewed the improvement in transportation solely as a means of bolstering their monoculture.

Whether one views the advent of the iron horse as being beneficial or detrimental to the South, one cannot deny that the railroad's impact on the southern economy was real and immediate. Southerners never again relied exclusively on river transportation. With the introduction of alternative commercial highways, new means of marketing cotton supplanted the old. On the verge of a civil war that would decimate the very foundation of the southern economic structure, the railroads had already conducted the South into a new age.

$\mathcal{N}otes$

# Introduction

1. Harold Woodman, "Economy from 1815 to 1865," in *Encyclopedia of American Economic History: Studies of the Principal Movements and Ideas,* ed. Glenn Porter, vol. 1 (New York: Scribner's, 1980), 68.

2. Ibid., 69.

3. Douglass C. North, *The Economic Growth of the United States, 1790–1860* (Englewood Cliffs, N.J.: Prentice-Hall, 1961), 68.

4. Stuart Bruchey, ed., *Cotton and the Growth of the American Economy: 1790–1860* (Atlanta: Harcourt, Brace, and World, 1967), 2.

5. U.S. Congress, Senate, *Report of Israel D. Andrews . . . on the Trade and Commerce of the British North American Colonies . . .* , Senate Executive Document 112, 32nd Cong., 1st sess., 1853, 834.

6. George Rogers Taylor, *The Transportation Revolution, 1815–1860,* vol. 4 of *The Economic History of the United States* (New York: Harper and Row, 1951).

7. Louis Hunter, *Steamboats on the Western Rivers: An Economic and Technological History* (Cambridge: Harvard University Press, 1943), 3–60.

8. Diane Lindstrom, "Domestic Trade and Regional Specialization," in *Encyclopedia of American Economic History,* ed. Glenn Porter, vol. 1:273.

9. Woodman, "Economy from 1815 to 1865," 77.

10. Lindstrom, "Domestic Trade and Regional Specialization," 273.

11. Woodman, "Economy from 1815 to 1865," 77.

12. Ibid., 79.

13. For more on the process by which these phenomena occurred, see Taylor, *The Transportation Revolution;* Thomas C. Cochran, *Business in American Life: A History* (New York: McGraw-Hill, 1972); Larry Schweikart, *Banking in the American South from the Age of Jackson to Reconstruction* (Baton Rouge: Louisiana State University Press, 1987); Elisha P. Douglass, *The Coming of Age of American Business: Three Centuries of Enterprise, 1600–1900* (Chapel Hill: University of North Carolina Press, 1971); and Robert William Fogel and Stanley L. Engerman, eds., *The Reinterpretation of American Economic History* (New York: Harper and Row, 1971).

14. John W. Stormont, *The Economics of Secession and Coercion, 1861* (Victoria, Tex.: Victoria Advocate Publishing Co., 1957), 57.

15. Ibid., 55.

16. *DeBow's Review,* 22 (January–June 1857): 543.

17. Peter A. Coclanis, *The Shadow of a Dream: Economic Life and Death in the South Carolina Low Country, 1670–1920* (New York: Oxford University Press, 1989).

# 1. A Cotton Economy

1. Harry P. Owens, "Apalachicola: The Beginning," *Florida Historical Quarterly* 47, no. 3 (January 1969): 279.

2. Florida Bureau of Land and Water Management, *The Apalachicola River and Bay System: A Florida Resource* ([Tallahassee]: F.B.L.W.M., 1977), 1.

3. *Apalachicola Gazette,* 29 January 1840.

4. George L. Chapel, "Walking and Driving Tour of Historic Apalachicola," Apalachicola Chamber of Commerce.

5. Harry P. Owens, "Apalachicola Before 1861" (Ph.D. diss., Florida State University, 1966), 115–33.

6. An 1838 territorial census taken "during the season" showed a population of more than four thousand. *Apalachicola Gazette,* 21 June 1838, reprinted in Rose Gibbons Lovett, "Excerpts and Articles Relating to Apalachicola and Area," 53, Lovett Family Papers, Florida State Archives, Tallahassee.

7. In the 1842–43 season, almost twenty-five hundred sailors arrived in Apalachicola. See Dorothy Dodd, *Apalachicola: Antebellum Cotton Port* ([Tallahassee]: privately published, n.d.), 7.

8. Quoted in Weymouth T. Jordan, *Ante-bellum Alabama: Town and Country* (Tallahassee: Florida State University, 1957; reprint, Tuscaloosa: University of Alabama Press, 1986), 21.

9. Raphael J. Moses Autobiography, Typescript, 40, Southern Historical Collection, University of North Carolina, Chapel Hill.

10. Niles Schuh, ed., "Apalachicola in 1838–1840: Letters from a Young Cotton Warehouse Clerk," *Florida Historical Quarterly* 68, no. 3 (January 1990): 318.

11. Apalachicola *Commercial Advertiser,* 30 November 1844, p. 2.

12. *Apalachicola Gazette,* 4 April 1840, reprinted in Lovett, "Excerpts and Articles," 5; *Commercial Advertiser Price Current,* 9 May 1853.

13. *Florida House Journal,* 1860, 14–17.

14. Apalachicola *Commercial Advertiser,* 13 June 1846, p. 3; *Commercial Advertiser Price Current,* 21 April 1851, in Gray Family Papers, Southern Historical Collection. In 1846 of the almost ninety-three thousand bales exported, only about thirty-three thousand went directly to foreign ports. About fifty-eight thousand bales were shipped coastwise. See *Commercial Advertiser,* 13 June 1846, p. 3. Woodman estimated that only one bale in five was actually consumed in the United States. See Harold D. Woodman, *King Cotton and His Retainers: Financing and Marketing the Cotton Crop of the South, 1800–1925* (Lexington: University of Kentucky Press, 1968), 28. For more detail on the destination of Apalachicola exports, see chapter two.

15. Owens, "Apalachicola Before 1861," 110.

16. Most were forcibly removed in 1837, but it was 1843 before it was announced that all the Indians had been removed. See ibid., 106.

17. George W. Featherstonhaugh, *Excursion Through the Slave States* (New York: Harper and Brothers, 1844), 320.

18. James S. Buckingham, *The Slave States of America,* 2 vols. (London: Fisher, Son and Co., 1842), 1:247.

19. Frederick Law Olmsted, *The Cotton Kingdom. A Traveller's Observations on Cotton and Slavery in the American Slave States,* ed. Arthur Schlesinger (New York: Alfred A. Knopf, 1953), 213; Buckingham, *The Slave States,* 244–46. Buckingham complained that he had arrived at the "*ne plus ultra* of disorder, neglect, and dirtiness," and Olmsted remarked he had seen no place but Washington where "so much gambling, intoxication, and cruel treatment of servants in public" could be found.

20. Lillian Foster, *Wayside Glimpses, North and South* (1860; reprint, New York: Negro Universities Press, 1969), 111–18; Gayle-Crawford Family Papers, vol. 6, 17 July 1853, Southern Historical Collection.

21. Columbus *Times*, 25 December 1844, quoted in *Inventory of County Archives of Georgia*, No. 106, Muscogee County (Atlanta: Georgia Historical Records Survey, 1941), 11; John H. Martin, comp., *Columbus, Geo., From Its Selection as a 'Trading Town' in 1827 to its Partial Destruction by Wilson's Raid in 1865* (1874; reprint, n.p.: Georgia Genealogical Reprints, 1972), Part I, 162. For Columbus receipts from 1840 to 1860, see Table 7-1.

22. Jeremy Atack, Fred Bateman, and Thomas Weiss, "Risk, the Rate of Return and the Pattern of Investment in Nineteenth Century American Manufacturing," *Southern Economic Journal* 49, no. 1 (July 1982): 150–63.

23. George White, *Statistics of the State of Georgia* (1849; reprint, Spartanburg, S.C.: Reprint Co., 1972), 446–48.

24. Martin, *Columbus, Geo.*, Part II, 119.

25. John Lupold, *Columbus, Georgia, 1828–1928* (Columbus: Columbus Sesquicentennial, 1978), 23.

26. *Columbus City Directory, 1859–1860* (Columbus: Sun Book and Job Printing Office, 1859), 77–86.

27. Owens, "Apalachicola: The Beginning," 289.

28. Owens, "Apalachicola Before 1861," 243.

29. Ibid., 109. For more on the founding of Columbus and the intrusion of whites onto Indian land throughout the valley, see Mary E. Young, *Redskins, Ruffleshirts, and Rednecks* (Norman: University of Oklahoma Press, 1961), 73–113.

30. Mrs. Marvin Scott, *History of Henry County, Alabama* (Pensacola: Frank R. Parkhurst and Son, 1961), 23, 27, 34, 43, 91, 93; Anne Kendrick Walker, *Russell County in Retrospect* (Richmond, Va.: Dietz Press, 1950), 176, 181.

31. See Joel W. Perry, comp., *Some Pioneer History of Early County*, (n.p.: n.d.), 26–31.

32. Apalachicola *Commercial Advertiser*, 8 January 1844, p. 4.

33. Clay County Library, *The History of Clay County* ([Fort Gaines, Ga.]: N.p., 1976), 7–8.

34. Woodman, *King Cotton*, 7.

35. Apalachicola *Commercial Advertiser*, 30 March 1844, p. 1; *Columbus Enquirer*, 11 October 1843, p. 3.

36. Albany *Patriot*, 1 December 1847, p. 4.

37. L. F. E. Dugas to T. Rogers and Company, 22 February 1845, L. F. E. Dugas Letterbook, Southern Historical Collection.

38. Norman Sydney Buck, *Anglo-American Trade, 1800–1850* (1925; reprint, New Haven: Yale University Press, 1969), 80.

39. See Niles Schuh private collection of Apalachicola business letters, Panama City, Florida; D. K. Dodge to Abraham Bell and Son, 3 January 1850, MS-22, and William T. Wood to S. Davol, 27 December 1845, MS-96, both in manuscript collection, Dorothy Dodd Room, Florida State Library, Tallahassee.

40. L. F. E. Dugas Letterbook, passim, Southern Historical Collection.

41. Advertisement of Rees and Butt in *Columbus Enquirer*, 7 December 1842, p. 3.

42. See advertisements in Apalachicola *Commercial Advertiser* and *Columbus Enquirer*, passim.

43. Fred Mitchell Jones, *Middlemen in the Domestic Trade of the United States, 1800–1860* (1937; reprint, New York: Johnson Reprint Corp., 1968), 27.

44. *DeBow's Review*, 10 (January–June 1851): 334.

45. David L. Cohn, *The Life and Times of King Cotton* (New York: Oxford University Press, 1956), 189.

46. T. S. Miller, Sr., *The American Cotton System Historically Treated Showing Operations of the Cotton Exchanges* (Austin: Austin Printing Co., 1909), 48. The Apalachicola and Columbus commercial reports occasionally mentioned three other classifications. There was occasionally some "Good fair" cotton in Apalachicola. Furthermore, there was a "Liverpool middling," and a "Strict Northern middling," the former being valued over Strict middling and the latter slightly higher than Liverpool middling. See *Columbus Enquirer*, 18 December 1858, p. 2, and 6 February 1858, p. 3.

47. Miller, *American Cotton System*, 48.

48. Ibid., 38.

49. William G. Porter and Company to David L. Barrow, 5 March 1859, Barrow Papers, Southern Historical Collection.

50. L. F. E. Dugas to Victor Poutz, 10 September 1844, Dugas Family Papers, Southern Historical Collection.

51. Albany *Patriot*, 22 December 1854, p. 2.

52. At least two Apalachicola factors charged fifty cents per bale as a selling commission. See John Horry Dent Papers, vol. 1, 179, Historic Chattahoochee Commission, Eufaula; *Columbus Enquirer*, 22 July 1851, p. 3; Harriet E. Amos, *Cotton City: Urban Development in Antebellum Mobile* (Tuscaloosa: University of Alabama Press, 1985), 29.

53. Alexander Allen to George W. Allen, 11 January 1855, G. W. Allen Papers, Southern Historical Collection.

54. Woodman, *King Cotton*, 71.

55. Robert J. Albion, "Foreign Trade in the Era of Wooden Ships," in Harold F. Williamson, ed., *The Growth of the American Economy: An Introduction to the Economic History of the United States* (New York: Prentice-Hall, 1944), 164.

56. Invoice of cotton sold by Wm. G. Porter and Company for account of J. W. Russ estate, 8 February 1848, William Bradley Collection, Florida State Archives, Tallahassee.

57. Charles S. Davis, *The Cotton Kingdom in Alabama* (Montgomery: Alabama State Department of Archives and History, 1939), 145; Julia Floyd Smith, *Slavery and Plantation Growth in Antebellum Florida, 1821–1860* (Gainesville: University of Florida Press, 1973), 156.

58. Reprinted in Albany *Patriot*, 20 April 1855, p. 2.

59. Cohn, *Life and Times of King Cotton*, 188.

60. Albany *Patriot*, 20 March 1856, p. 2.

61. Martin, *Columbus. Geo.*, II, 19. An 1861 map of Columbus shows the Lowell Cotton Warehouse located on the riverfront. See George J. Burrus Map, Southern Historical Collection.

62. Brown Brothers and Company, Ledger Accounts, passim, New York Public Library, New York City. These accounts show many dealings with commission merchants in Apalachicola and Columbus, but also with firms in Eufaula and Marianna.

63. Paris J. Tillinghast to Samuel W. Tillinghast, 19 August 1844, William Norwood Tillinghast Papers, Southern Historical Collection.

64. Ibid., 23 June 1846.

65. Ibid., 19 June 1852.

66. Complaint, Nourse, Stone and Company, *v.* Oliver and Paris Tillinghast, 25 July 1853, Georgia Supreme Court Case A-1197, Georgia Archives, Atlanta. It was common for factors to finance buyers who then speculated on their own account. See Harold D. Woodman, "Itinerant Cotton Merchants of the Antebellum South," *Agricultural History* 40, no. 2 (April 1966): 88–89.

67. Paris J. Tillinghast to Samuel W. Tillinghast, 21 January 1854.

68. Edwin J. Perkins, *Financing Anglo-American Trade: The House of Brown, 1800–1888* (Cambridge, Mass., and London: Harvard University Press, 1975), 46.

69. Paris Tillinghast to Samuel Tillinghast, 23 June 1845 and 23 June 1846.

70. B. A. Sorsby advertisement in *Columbus Enquirer*, 5 October 1842, p. 3; Thom and Hardin advertisement in Columbus *Times*, 9 September 1841, p. 3.

71. See Owens, "Apalachicola Before 1861," 243. There were 7,436 farms of less than one hundred acres, 4,124 of from one hundred to five hundred, 745 of from five hundred to one thousand, and 222 of over one thousand acres.

72. Lewis E. Atherton, *The Southern Country Store, 1800–1860* (1949; reprint, New York: Greenwood Press, 1968), 12–14.

73. Ibid.

74. J. N. Copeland and Company, Invoice Book, in basement of the Clayton, Alabama, Courthouse.

75. Terry Family Papers, Southern Historical Collection.

76. "Warehouse Ledger A" (1846–1848), in Clay County Courthouse vault, Fort Gaines, Georgia.

77. Buck, *Anglo-American Trade,* 17–18; Thomas Moore Commonplace Book, p. 316, Manuscript Department, William R. Perkins Library, Duke University.

78. Jones, *Middlemen in the Domestic Trade,* 28–29.

79. Apalachicola *Watchman of the Gulf,* 12 August 1843, passim.

80. *Columbus City Directory, 1859–1860,* passim.

81. Apalachicola *Gazette,* 4 July 1836, p. 3. Upriver at Eufaula the E. and W. Young firm charged 3.5 percent for the same service. See Dent Plantation Record, vol. 1, 99.

82. Charles Rogers to Caleb Hopkins, 30 November 1838, in Miscellaneous Letters, Box 37, P. K. Yonge Library of Florida History, University of Florida, Gainesville.

83. See advertisements in Apalachicola *Commercial Advertiser,* passim; W. A. and P. C. Kain to A. R. Johnston, 2 March and 16 March 1847, in Miscellaneous Letters, Box 37, P. K. Yonge Library; John C. Maclay Shipping Record, in Gloria Tucker Private Collection, Apalachicola, Florida.

84. Advertisements of Edward J. Hardin in *Columbus Enquirer,* 25 September 1844 and 23 September 1846, both on p. 1.

85. Bertha S. Dodge, *Cotton: The Plant That Would Be King* (Austin: University of Texas Press, 1984), 119; M. B. Hammond, *The Cotton Industry, An Essay in American Economic History* (1897; reprint, New York: Johnson Reprint Corp., 1966), 113.

86. Lovett, "Excerpts and Articles," 13.

87. U.S. Congress, *Seventh Census, 1850,* Industry schedule, Franklin County, 201.

88. "An ordinance prohibiting persons who are not appointed weigh masters of the city of Apalachicola from weighing cotton offered for sale in city," in Lovett Papers, Box 2, Florida State Archives; William A. Kain to

Gov. W. D. Moseley, 30 December 1845, Record Group 101, Series 679, Box 1, Folder 1, Florida State Archives, Tallahassee.

89. Apalachicola *Commercial Advertiser*, 22 January 1844, p. 2; Smith, *Slavery and Plantation Growth*, 168.

90. Apalachicola *Commercial Advertiser*, 16 March 1848, p. 3.

91. Columbus *Times*, 27 June 1848, p. 4; *Columbus Enquirer*, 7 March 1848, p. 4, 4 October 1843, p. 3; Apalachicola *Commercial Advertiser*, 5 January 1844, p. 3, 8 January 1844, p. 5, 1 June 1848, p. 3. Only two companies were owned by southerners: the Southern Mutual Insurance Company in Columbus and the Augusta Insurance and Banking Company in Apalachicola. See Columbus *Times*, 18 April 1848, p. 4; *Commercial Advertiser*, 5 February 1844, p. 3.

92. Apalachicola *Commercial Advertiser*, 15 January 1844, p. 3. This same agent advertised that he was agent of another company that handled "river risks." See ibid.

93. Guion and Collins to George Gray, 24 May 1851, Gray Family Papers.

94. Advertisement of Harper and Owens, in *Spirit of the South*, 16 October 1855, p. 4.

95. C. C. Yonge collected eighteen dollars and received a fee of five dollars. See John B. Davis to C. C. Yonge, 8 May 1849, Chandler C. Yonge Papers, Box 3, Florida Collection, P. K. Yonge Library.

96. The Mercantile Agency to William E. Smith, 1 December 1854, in William Ephram Smith Papers, Manuscript Department, William R. Perkins Library, Duke University.

97. R. G. Dun Collection, passim, Baker Library, Harvard Business School, Harvard University.

## 2. Apalachicola Aweigh

1. In addition to the two lights at Apalachicola, the other north Florida lighthouses were located at St. Marks, St. Joseph's, and Pensacola. See the nautical map by E. and G. W. Blunt, "The North Coast of the Gulf of Mexico from St. Marks to Galveston" (New York: Chas. Copley, 1844) at the Phillips Library, Peabody Museum, Salem, Massachusetts.

2. See Log of the bark *Gleaner*, 4 February 1843–3 April 1844; Log of ship *Moro Castle*, 23 February 1860–17 January 1861; Journal of Mrs. Henry Moulton aboard the bark *Kepler*, 14 October 1859–20 March 1860;

Log of ship *Sarah Parker*, 28 January 1837–31 January 1840; Log of ship *Henry Ware*, 11 March 1851–29 November 1851. All of the above are located in the Phillips Library at Peabody Museum, Salem, Massachusetts.

3. The city's residents in 1840 and 1850 numbered just over one thousand. See U.S. Congress, *Sixth Census, 1840* (Washington, D.C.: Blair and Rives, 1841), Franklin County, Florida; U.S. Congress, *Seventh Census, 1850*, Franklin County, Florida.

4. Harry P. Owens, "Apalachicola Before 1861" (Ph.D. diss., Florida State University, 1966), 165–67, 173; Apalachicola *Star of the West*, 25 October 1848, p. 4.

5. See "Marine Intelligence," in Apalachicola *Commercial Advertiser*, 1 January–30 June 1844, passim. The extant Apalachicola papers are so scattered that the only shipping season in which a continuous run of newspapers exist is January through July 1844. Therefore, this chapter will rely heavily on data from that season.

6. Apalachicola *Commercial Advertiser*, 8 January 1844, p. 3, gave the 1842–43 statistics. For the 1844–45 season see Rose Gibbons Lovett, "Excerpts and Articles Relating to Apalachicola and Area," 16, in Lovett Family Papers, Florida State Archives, Tallahassee. Lovett quotes from *Niles Register*, 7 February 1846.

7. Robert Greenhalgh Albion, *Square-Riggers on Schedule: The New York Sailing Packets to England, France, and Cotton Ports* (1938; reprint, Hamden, Conn.: Archon Books, 1965), 11.

8. Robert Greenhalgh Albion, *The Rise of New York Port, 1815–1860* (New York: Charles Scribner's Sons, 1939), 271, 412.

9. Albion, *Square-Riggers*, 11; Apalachicola *Commercial Advertiser*, 14 December 1844, p. 2.

10. *Hunt's Merchants Magazine*, 28 (January–June 1853): 247.

11. In 1859 forty-seven vessels were licensed as wreckers there. See *De-Bow's Review*, 26 (January–June 1859): 219.

12. Entry of 23 February 1860, Log of ship *Moro Castle*, Phillips Library, Peabody Museum.

13. Entries for 4–7 March 1860, ibid.

14. Entry of 6 March 1860, ibid.

15. Entry of 8 March 1860, ibid.

16. Entry of 9 March 1860, ibid.

17. Entry of 10 March 1860, ibid. Apalachicola was often spelled with two "p's" in the nineteenth century.

18. Entries of 10–16 March 1860, ibid.

19. The Moultons were in Apalachicola from 26 January 1860 to 21 March 1860. See Journal kept by Mrs. Henry Moulton of the bark *Kepler*, 14 October 1859–20 March 1860, Phillips Library, Peabody Museum.

20. Entries of 3 February and 3 March 1860, ibid.

21. Entries of 6, 7, 13 March 1860, ibid.

22. See logs of ships *Henry Ware* and *Sarah Parker*, Phillips Library, Peabody Museum.

23. Very few steam-powered vessels came into Apalachicola before the Civil War. The Apalachicola newspaper noted only four oceangoing steamers entering the port in 1844. During the 1850s at various times three steamers made regular stops at Apalachicola and other Gulf ports.

24. John and Alice Durant, *Pictorial History of American Ships on the High Seas and Inland Waters* (New York: A. S. Barnes, 1953), 42.

25. "Vessels in Port," in Apalachicola *Commercial Advertiser*, 1 January–31 June 1844, passim.

26. Statistics on arrivals and departures of all types of vessels were compiled from the "Marine Intelligence" column in the weekly *Commercial Advertiser*, 1 January–31 June 1844.

27. Durant, *Pictorial History of American Ships*, 43. The average bark that served Apalachicola in 1844 was 364 tons.

28. Nineteen percent of the barks departing from Apalachicola in that season cleared for Liverpool, and 17 percent went to Boston.

29. Albion, *Square-Riggers*, 13. In 1844 the ships calling on Apalachicola were on average 432 tons.

30. When other European ports are included with the Liverpool figures, one finds that 14 percent of the brigs, barks, and ships leaving Apalachicola in 1844 sailed directly to European ports.

31. Albion, *Square-Riggers*, 20, 38.

32. Direct shipments to Liverpool averaged 31 percent.

33. Albion, *Square-Riggers*, 60.

34. Harriet E. Amos, *Cotton City: Urban Development in Antebellum Mobile* (Tuscaloosa: University of Alabama Press, 1985), 24.

35. Diane Lindstrom, "Domestic Trade and Regional Specialization," in *Encyclopedia of American Economic History: Studies of the Principal Movements and Ideas*, ed. Glenn Porter, vol. 1 (New York: Scribner's, 1980), 271.

36. Data collected from "Marine Intelligence" column of the weekly *Commercial Advertiser* for the months of January through June 1844.

37. The only other Apalachicola exports to New Orleans during the

1843–44 commercial season amounted to 150 sacks of cotton seed, 16 bales of cotton fabric, 3 bales of gunny bags, 238 sacks of coffee, and 25 cords of firewood. The piece goods were undoubtedly manufactured in Columbus, Georgia, at the head of river navigation. See Apalachicola *Commercial Advertiser,* 1 January–31 June 1844, passim.

38. Robert Norris Accounts, Manuscript Department, William R. Perkins Library, Duke University.

39. Norris began and ended each shipping season in New York. Luckily for him, the cotton cargoes from Apalachicola to New York were so profitable that together with the proceeds from the New Orleans to Apalachicola runs, the vessel earned $2834.98 in 1851.

40. See Table 2-2.

41. Charles Rogers to Francis C. Lowell, 6 April 1839, and Thomas L. Mitchel to C. H. Dabney, 23 February 1843. Both letters are in Niles Schuh Private Collection, Panama City, Florida.

42. Samuel Eliot Morison, *Maritime History of Massachusetts, 1783–1860* (Boston: Houghton Mifflin Co., 1941), 228.

43. This figure was derived by adding all the cotton exports listed by vessel in the *Commercial Advertiser* between 1 January and 30 June 1844.

44. Havana was the only destination to which no cotton was ever exported. The Cuban port supplied groceries to Apalachicola, and return vessels from Florida carried only empty containers.

45. Apalachicola *Commercial Advertiser,* 8 January 1844, p. 3.

46. I use the term "western" to encompass goods raised in the border states as well. Although there is much interest among some economic historians as to whether "western" products were actually grown in the western states, that issue is beyond the scope of this inquiry, and, therefore, when used in this context refers to any commodities raised or made outside the Cotton South but which passed through New Orleans.

47. Louis Bernard Schmidt, "Internal Commerce and the Development of the National Economy," *Journal of Political Economy* 47 (December 1939): 798–822; Douglass C. North, *The Economic Growth of the United States, 1790–1860* (Englewood Cliffs, N.J.: Prentice-Hall, 1961), 101–103.

48. Robert E. Gallman, "Self-Sufficiency in the Cotton Economy of the Antebellum South," in *The Structure of the Cotton Economy of the Antebellum South,* ed. William N. Parker (Baltimore: Waverly Press, 1970), 5–24; Diane Lindstrom, "Southern Dependence Upon Interregional Grain Supplies: A Review of the Trade Flows, 1840–1860," in ibid., 101–13; Albert Fishlow, *American Railroads and the Transformation of the Ante-Bellum*

*Economy* (Cambridge: Harvard University Press, 1965), reprinted in part in Stuart Bruchey, ed., *Cotton and the Growth of the American Economy: 1790–1860* (Atlanta: Harcourt, Brace, and World, 1967), 98–107.

49. The population total is taken from U.S. Congress, *Sixth Census, 1840*, passim. The counties that relied on the river for transportation included the Florida counties of Jackson, Washington, Calhoun, Franklin, and Gadsden. Alabama counties bordering the river included Henry, Barbour, and Russell. The Georgia counties were Baker, Decatur, Dooly, Early, Harris, Lee, Marion, Muscogee, Stewart, Sumter, and Talbot. Altogether, the population of the river valley in 1840, including slaves, equaled 146,160.

50. See Table 2-3 for Apalachicola imports. This calculation assumes that a barrel of meat weighed 200 pounds. Bacon, listed separately in ships manifests, was not included in the above calculation because it was often shipped in casks of varying measure. Yet the 214 casks and 14 hogsheads of bacon that Apalachicola imported in that season would not have gone far in a population of 146,000.

51. The Irish potato, which eventually became a southern staple, was originally grown only in New England because it was believed the crop could be cultivated only in cold climates. After 1850 the potato was commonly grown in Georgia, but the southern variety had a tendency to rot and, therefore, was not marketable. See James C. Bonner, *A History of Georgia Agriculture, 1732–1860* (Athens: University of Georgia Press, 1964), 168. In the 1844 season, more than 68,000 pounds of potatoes were imported into Apalachicola.

52. Albion, *Square-Riggers*, 71; George Rogers Taylor, *The Transportation Revolution, 1815–1860* (New York: Harper and Row, 1951), 170. Near the western end of Dog Island is Ballast Cove where ballast rocks were once unloaded after coming into St. George Sound. When anchored there in the early 1980s, the author noted a pile of rocks not native to Florida half-buried in the sand.

53. Edward B. Jenkins to Thomas C. Lennan, 3 June 1840, in Manuscript Box 37, P. K. Yonge Library, University of Florida, Gainesville.

54. E. B. Mallet to "Friend Thomas," 15 March 1852, Box 15, P. K. Yonge Library.

55. Because it was unlawful in Florida for free blacks to enter the state, the captain of any boat that had black crew members had to post bond and pay any expenses incurred in jailing them. Because this practice was bad for business, local merchants petitioned the state assembly in 1849 to amend the law. The resulting legislation stated that boats having free Negroes

aboard must anchor no nearer to Apalachicola than five miles, and no communication between them and the crews of other vessels was allowed. See Apalachicola *Commercial Advertiser,* 4 January 1849, p. 2, and 25 January 1849, p. 2.

56. Edward Marshall to William Rice, 1 March 1843, in Niles Schuh private collection.

57. Robert Norris Accounts, Manuscript Department, William R. Perkins Library, Duke University.

58. The movements of vessels calling on Apalachicola were noted in the Apalachicola *Commercial Advertiser,* 1 January–30 June 1844, passim.

59. Lovett, "Excerpts and Articles," p. 56, quoting the *Apalachicola Gazette,* 21 March 1840.

60. Apalachicola *Commercial Advertiser,* 23 November 1844, p. 3.

61. The steam propeller *Florida* came down from New York in 1844. See Apalachicola *Commercial Advertiser,* 21 December 1844, p. 2.

62. *Columbus Enquirer,* 9 November 1852, p. 3.

63. Columbus *Times and Sentinel,* 31 January 1854, p. 2.

64. *Columbus Enquirer,* 24 October 1854, p. 4.

65. Apalachicola *Commercial Advertiser,* 10 March 1858, p. 2.

66. Albany *Patriot,* 28 May 1857, p. 2; Apalachicola *Commercial Advertiser,* 10 March 1858, p. 2.

67. *Columbus Enquirer,* 22 June 1858, p. 2. It is not known whether the "Apalachicola and New Orleans Steam Navigation Company" ever began operations.

68. *Columbus Enquirer,* 14 April 1842, p. 1, and 28 September 1842, p. 3.

69. Amos, *Cotton City,* 22.

70. Lovett, "Excerpts and Articles," 22. The price of passage was forty dollars, excluding liquors, and all the vessels were coppered and copper fastened.

71. Apalachicola *Commercial Advertiser,* 9 September 1844, p. 3. The ships *Uncas* and *Emblem* were never mentioned in the *Commercial Advertiser's* marine intelligence.

72. Albion, *Square-Riggers,* 59, 70; Amos, *Cotton City,* 22.

73. Albion, *Square-Riggers,* 60.

74. The only exception was the ship *Tuskina,* which was owned by Hurlbut, but not advertised as being a line ship. It had formerly been a New York/Mobile packet, but sailed the "cotton triangle" after 1839. In the fall of 1844, it arrived in Apalachicola from New York and cleared for Liverpool.

75. Apalachicola *Commercial Advertiser,* 9 November 1844, p. 1.

76. Albion, *Square-Riggers*, 20, 38.

77. These were the barks *Alabama, Colossus,* and *Mersey,* and the ships *Blanchard, Charlemagne,* and *Manco.* See Apalachicola *Commercial Advertiser,* 1844, passim.

78. Apalachicola *Commercial Advertiser,* 14 February 1846, p. 2.

79. Apalachicola *Commercial Advertiser,* 23 May 1846, p. 3, 6 February 1847, p. 3; Entries of April 1859, of ship *Eliza Morrison,* in J. C. Maclay Shipping Register, 1858–1861, in possession of Mrs. Gloria Tucker, Apalachicola.

80. Going freight rates were published weekly in the Apalachicola *Commercial Advertiser,* 1844, passim. These quotations were listed as so many cents or pence per pound. The above calculations assumed the average bale weighed five hundred pounds. The pence was the equivalent of two cents. See *Merchants' Magazine* 3 (July–December 1840): 264; T. S. Miller, Sr., *The American Cotton System Historically Treated Showing Operations of the Cotton Exchanges* (Austin: Austin Printing Co., 1909), 273. Prices declined slightly with time as technology improved. See Taylor, *The Transportation Revolution,* 148.

81. Apalachicola *Commercial Advertiser,* 7 July 1846, p. 2; Log of bark *Kepler,* 26 January to 21 March 1860.

82. Apalachicola *Commercial Advertiser,* 25 October 1844, p. 2, 31 October 1846, p. 2.

83. Columbus *Times,* 4 March 1841, p. 2.

84. *Hunts Merchants' Magazine,* 43 (July–December 1860): 96.

85. Ibid.

86. Insurance charges depended on whether the craft was sailing northward or southward and whether or not it was hurricane season. See *Merchants' Magazine,* 3 (July–December 1840): 169; Albion, *Rise of New York Port,* 412.

## 3. Cotton Money

1. Larry Schweikart, *Banking in the American South from the Age of Jackson to Reconstruction* (Baton Rouge: Louisiana State University Press, 1987), 5–6.

2. Peter Temin, *The Jacksonian Economy* (New York: W. W. Norton, 1969), 89–90.

3. Neil Carothers, *Fractional Money* (1930; reprint, New York: A. M. Kelly, 1967), 22.

4. Ibid., 25–26.

5. Ibid., 34–35.

6. Ibid., 148.

7. Ibid., 34–35.

8. Thomas Joseph Peddy, "Reminiscences of Columbus by John E. Lamar," Handbound typescript, 1984, W. C. Bradley Memorial Library, Columbus, 35.

9. Ibid.

10. *Merchants' Magazine* 17 (July–December 1847): 429.

11. Carothers, *Fractional Money,* 78.

12. *Columbus Enquirer,* 22 June 1849, p. 2.

13. Carothers, *Fractional Money,* 95.

14. Brokers were selling new gold coins at 8 percent premium in 1849. See Ritchie to Murdock, 18 May 1849, Murdock-Wright Papers, Southern Historical Collection, University of North Carolina.

15. William H. Dilliston, *Bank Note Reporters and Counterfeit Detectors, 1826–1866* (New York: American Numismatic Society, 1949), 66.

16. In 1846 the Columbus *Times* reported that responsible merchants were accepting them from their customers, but, instead of paying them out, they were taking them back to the originator for redemption. Columbus *Times,* 1 April 1846, p. 2.

17. Ibid., 25 November 1841, p. 3.

18. *Columbus Enquirer,* 14 December 1842, p. 3.

19. Ibid., 2 August 1843, p. 3.

20. Ibid., 9 November 1842, p. 3.

21. Ibid., 28 September 1842, p. 3.

22. Ibid.

23. Ibid., 14 December 1842, p. 3.

24. Private shinplasters were listed along with local bank notes in the report of the local money market although the local banks claimed they would not take them. See *Columbus Enquirer,* 29 November 1843, p. 3.

25. John H. Martin, comp., *Columbus Geo., From Its Selection as a 'Trading Town' in 1827 to its Partial Destruction by Wilson's Raid in 1865,* Part II (1874; reprint, N.p.: Georgia Genealogical Reprints, 1972), 13.

26. Davis R. Dewey, *State Banking Before the Civil War* (Washington, D.C.: U.S. Government Printing Office, 1910), 64.

27. Columbus *Times,* 18 July 1848, p. 2.

28. Daniel G. Cassidy, *The Illustrated History of Florida Paper Money* (Jacksonville, Fla.: Mendelson Printing and Office Supply Co., 1980), 37;

Harley L. Freeman, *Florida Obsolete Notes and Scrip* (N.p.: Society of Paper Money Collectors, 1967), 11.

29. Dewey, *State Banking*, 149.

30. William H. Brantley, *Banking in Alabama, 1837–1849* (Birmingham, Ala.: Oxmoor Press, 1967), 2:19.

31. Dewey, *State Banking*, 68, 73.

32. Cassidy, *Illustrated History of Florida Paper Money*, 30, 33; Raphael J. Moses, Autobiography, 42, Southern Historical Collection, University of North Carolina.

33. T. Joe Peddy, "Reminiscences of Columbus," unnumbered; Cassidy, *Illustrated History of Florida Paper Money*, 33.

34. Columbus *Times*, 18 February 1846, p. 3. The editor reasoned that if Winter died, the bills would not be redeemable.

35. Ibid., 4 March 1846, p. 2.

36. Ibid.

37. *Acts of the General Assembly of the State of Georgia, 1835* (Milledgeville: John A. Cuthbert, 1836), 33–34.

38. Albany *Patriot*, 14 January 1853, p. 2.

39. *Acts of the General Assembly of the State of Georgia, 1851–52* (Macon: Samuel J. Ray, State Printer, 1852), 25–26.

40. See Albany *Patriot*, 4 February 1858, p. 2, in which the editor remarked of the legislation, that since the banks "could get no better terms from the Legislature of Georgia, whilst other States passed greatly more favorable laws . . . [this was] in itself sufficient to brand with falsehood, the disgusting insinuations, which we hear constantly made against the honor and honesty of . . . [the legislature]."

41. Raphael J. Moses, Autobiography, Southern Historical Collection, University of North Carolina, 42–43; The Bank of St. Mary's *v.* The State of Georgia, in *Reports of Cases in Law and Equity Argued and Determined in the Supreme Court of the State of Georgia* (Athens: Christy and Kelsea, 1853), 12:475–500.

42. *Columbus Enquirer*, 29 November 1843, p. 3.

43. Ibid., 27 October 1857, p. 2.

44. Reprinted from *Columbus Enquirer-Sun*, 18 October 1891, in Peddy, "Reminiscences of Columbus," 35.

45. Columbus *Times*, 25 November 1841, p. 3.

46. *Columbus Enquirer*, 15 March, 11 October 1843, 24 April 1844, 15 October 1845, all on p. 3.

47. Cassidy, *Illustrated History of Florida Paper Money*, 30, 33. Note that the values of the scrip corresponded to those of Spanish coins.

48. William Erwin, "Good Paper Money, Nothing Else Will Do," Duke University Newsletter, n.s., 31 (October 1983): 20.

49. Paul B. Trescott, *Financing American Enterprise: The Story of Commercial Banking* (New York: Harper and Row, 1963), 21.

50. *Columbus Enquirer,* 22 April 1851, p. 3.

51. A. Barton Hepburn, *A History of Currency in the United States* (1903; reprint, New York: Augustus M. Kelley, 1967), 165.

52. Cassidy, *Illustrated History of Florida Paper Money,* 26–35; Freeman, *Florida Obsolete Notes,* 3–10.

53. *Columbus Enquirer,* 5 February 1850, p. 2; *Albany Patriot,* 22 February 1850, p. 3.

54. Dilliston, *Bank Note Reporters,* 19.

55. Columbus *Times,* 6 May 1846, p. 2.

56. Dilliston, *Bank Note Reporters,* 16.

57. Ibid., 41. *Bicknell's Counterfeit Detector and Bank Note List* of January 1839 listed "1395 descriptions of counterfeited and altered notes then supposed to be in circulation." See George Rogers Taylor, *The Transportation Revolution, 1815–1860* (New York: Harper and Row, 1951), 326.

58. The manuals could either "puff" a bank (to claim that it was sound when it was not), or they might receive hush money not to "blow" a bank (to relate its worthlessness). Dilliston, *Bank Note Reporters,* 47–50.

59. Trescott, *Financing American Enterprise,* 21.

60. This original use of the term "carpetbagger" predates the Reconstruction period. Dilliston, *Bank Note Reporters,* 63; *The American Banker,* 21 June 1899, 1095.

61. Dilliston, *Bank Note Reporters,* 63.

62. Trescott, *Financing American Enterprise,* 21.

63. Ibid., 64.

64. Letter to J. Day and Company, 5 October 1849, Miscellaneous Southern Business Letters, Southern Historical Collection, University of North Carolina. It was not apparent from the letter where the bank bills originated, but the agent had just come from the North.

65. Taylor, *Transportation Revolution,* 326; Dilliston, *Bank Note Reporters,* 69; Cassidy, *Illustrated History of Florida Paper Money,* 32.

66. Herman E. Kroos and Martin B. Blyn, *A History of Financial Intermediaries* (New York: Random House, 1971), 28.

67. Columbus *Times,* 24 June 1841, p. 3.

68. *Columbus Enquirer,* 3 August 1842, p. 3.

69. Apalachicola *Watchman of the Gulf,* 12 August 1843, p. 4.

70. *Columbus Enquirer,* 11 October 1843, p. 3.

71. Memorial from the citizens of Apalachicola, dated 9 December 1848, reprinted in Julia Floyd Smith, *Slavery and Plantation Growth in Antebellum Florida, 1821–1860* (Gainesville: University of Florida Press, 1973), 169.

72. *Apalachicolian*, 26 December 1840, p. 3.

73. Ibid.

74. Lewis E. Atherton, *The Southern Country Store, 1800–1860* (1949; reprint, New York: Greenwood Press, 1968), 179.

75. *Commercial Advertiser*, passim.

76. See Thomas Gaulding to C. C. Yonge, 13 June 1846, C. C. Yonge Papers, P. K. Yonge Library, University of Florida, Gainesville, and Alexander A. Allen to George W. Allen, 20 February 1850, George Washington Allen Papers, Southern Historical Collection, University of North Carolina, Chapel Hill.

77. J. R. McCulloch, *A Dictionary, Practical, Theoretical, and Historical, of Commerce and Commercial Navigation* (London: A. Spotteswoode, 1839), 558.

78. Ibid., 564.

79. *Bankers' Magazine*, 10, New Series, No. 7, (January 1861): 565.

80. Apalachicola *Commercial Advertiser*, 14 October 1844, p. 3.

81. When a person deposited money in a bank, he received in return a certificate stating that this money had been placed to his credit. This certificate was payable to either the depositor or his order. The holder of the certificate could endorse it and pass it to his creditor or sell it to someone else requiring currency in the same locality as the bank. See Amasa Walker, *The Nature and Uses of Money and Mixed Currency with a History of the Wickaboag Bank* (Boston: Crosby, Nichols and Co., 1857), 22.

82. See John Horry Dent Papers, 4:65, 77, Historic Chattahoochee Commission, Eufaula.

83. Thomas P. Govan, "Banking and the Credit System in Georgia, 1810–1860," *Journal of Southern History* 4 (May 1938): 179–80; Paris J. Tillinghast to Samuel W. Tillinghast, 1 June 1841, William Norwood Tillinghast Papers, Manuscript Department, William R. Perkins Library, Duke University; L. F. E. Dugas to Thomas McGrau, 21 February 1845, and L. F. E. Dugas to A. P. Pilot, 23 February 1845, L. F. E. Letterbook, Southern Historical Collection, University of North Carolina, Chapel Hill.

84. Letter to Mrs. Sarah Cantrell, 6 March 1838, in Falconar Papers, Library of Maryland History, Maryland Historical Society, Baltimore.

## 4. Cotton Banks

1. Richard Sylla, "American Banking and Growth in the Nineteenth Century: A Partial View of the Terrain," *Explorations in Economic History* 9, no. 2 (Winter 1971/72): 221.

2. Sidney Ratner, James H. Soltow, and Richard Sylla, *The Evolution of the American Economy: Growth, Welfare, and Decision Making* (New York: Basic Books, 1979), 102.

3. Herman E. Kroos and Martin B. Blyn, *A History of Financial Intermediaries* (New York: Random House, 1971), 32.

4. Approximately two-thirds of all the land in Georgia was opened for white settlement in the 1820s and 1830s. See Milton Sydney Heath, *Constructive Liberalism: The Role of the State in Economic Development in Georgia to 1860* (Cambridge: Harvard University Press, 1954), 205.

5. Sylla, "American Banking and Growth in the Nineteenth Century," 211–20; Larry Schweikart, *Banking in the American South from the Age of Jackson to Reconstruction* (Baton Rouge: Louisiana State University Press, 1987), 225–66.

6. Ratner, Soltow, and Sylla, *Evolution of the American Economy,* 167; Peter Temin, *The Jacksonian Economy* (New York: W. W. Norton, 1969), 80–90, 92.

7. Temin, *The Jacksonian Economy,* 137–41.

8. Ibid., 115.

9. Ibid., 141–43, 152–54.

10. Heath, *Constructive Liberalism,* 207; *Columbus Enquirer,* 10 March 1841, p. 2.

11. E. J. Donnell, *Chronological and Statistical History of Cotton* (New York: James Sutton and Co., 1872), 282, 284, 296.

12. *Columbus Enquirer,* 28 April 1841, p. 2.

13. Paris Tillinghast to Samuel Tillinghast, 12 July 1841, William Norwood Tillinghast Papers, Manuscript Department, William R. Perkins Library, Duke University.

14. Hines Holt to Farish Carter, 28 March 1841, Farish Carter Papers, Southern Historical Collection, University of North Carolina, Chapel Hill.

15. Ibid.

16. Richard H. Long to Farish Carter, 7 May 1842, Carter Papers.

17. *Columbus Enquirer,* 26 January 1842, p. 2.

18. Ibid.

19. Paris Tillinghast to Samuel Tillinghast, 1 June 1841, Tillinghast Papers.

20. An 1841 Georgia statute required the banks to resume specie payments in February 1841 or forfeit their charter. The banks did resume specie payments in February, but suspended again in May. Columbus *Times,* 12 August 1841, p. 3.

21. *Columbus Enquirer,* 28 April 1841, p. 2.

22. Columbus *Times,* 12 August 1841, p. 3.

23. Heath, *Constructive Liberalism,* 221.

24. Kroos and Blyn, *History of Financial Intermediaries,* 25.

25. Ibid.

26. *Columbus Enquirer,* 29 April 1856, p. 2.

27. U.S. Congress, House of Representatives, *Condition of the State Banks,* House Document 226, 29th Cong., 1st sess., 677–78.

28. *Columbus Enquirer,* 29 April 1856, p. 2.

29. In 1840 Georgia explicitly forbade banks to deal in cotton as security for loans. See Davis R. Dewey, *State Banking Before the Civil War* (Washington, D.C.: U.S. Government Printing Office, 1910), 48.

30. Columbus *Times,* 15 July 1841, p. 2.

31. Ibid., 22 July 1841, p. 2.

32. Ibid., 11 March 1841, p. 2.

33. Ibid.

34. Paris Tillinghast to Samuel Tillinghast, 7 April 1841, Tillinghast Papers.

35. Fred R. Marckhoff, "The Development of Currency and Banking in Florida," *Coin Collector's Journal* (September–October 1947), 121.

36. Ibid.

37. The farther away the notes were circulated, the less probability that they would return for redemption. David Yancey Thomas, "A History of Banking in Florida," Typed manuscript, Special Collections, Robert Manning Strozier Library, Florida State University, 28.

38. Resolution to the Florida Legislative Council, signed by William G. Porter and H. R. Taylor (both prominent Apalachicola cotton factors), in Franklin County Papers, Florida Collection, Florida State Library.

39. The St. Augustine office never actively operated. The Florida bank committee of 1837 remarked that although the bank claimed to be operated in St. Augustine, its business was conducted chiefly in New York. See Thomas, "A History of Banking in Florida," 78.

40. Ibid., 26.

41. Ibid., 89–90.

42. Ibid., 27. In practice the loan was paid out in the depreciated bills of other banks. This practice caused a hardship on the borrower because these same depreciated bills were not necessarily accepted at their face value when the loan was repaid. See ibid., 74.

43. Ibid., 28.

44. Ibid.

45. Ibid., 78.

46. Governor's message on state of Florida banks, in House Document 111, 26th Cong., 2nd sess., 242.

47. Marckhoff, "Development of Currency and Banking," 121.

48. Southern Life Insurance and Trust Company annual statements, in *Journal of Florida Legislative Council,* 1840, unnumbered; Florida *House and Senate Journal,* 1841, Appendix, xvi.

49. See Amasa Walker, *The Nature and Uses of Money and Mixed Currency with a History of the Wickaboag Bank* (Boston: Crosby, Nichols and Co., 1857), 56.

50. J. R. McCulloch, *A Dictionary, Practical, Theoretical, and Historical, of Commerce and Commercial Navigation* (London: A. Spotteswoode, 1839), 538. If the Apalachicola merchant was in no hurry for his money, he deposited the bill of exchange at the bank for collection. On or before the due date, the bank notified the remitter that he could pay off the note there. Usually banks did not charge for this service in the hope that the money would remain in the bank on deposit.

51. Statements of the Bank of St. Mary's in *Columbus Enquirer,* 8 December 1846, p. 3, 9 November 1847, p. 3, 25 April 1848, p. 3; Albany *Patriot,* 8 November 1850, p. 3; Statement of the Bank of Columbus, in Albany *Patriot,* 23 April 1857, p. 2; Statement of the Bank of Brunswick, in *Columbus Enquirer,* 1 May 1849, p. 3.

52. Thomas, "History of Banking in Florida," 74; *Florida House and Senate Journal,* 1841, Appendix, xvi.

53. Dewey, *State Banking,* 180.

54. The legal interest rate in Florida was 8 percent. Columbus *Times,* 22 July 1846, p. 2.

55. Walker, *Nature and Uses of Money,* 59.

56. Dewey, *State Banking,* 168.

57. Thomas, "History of Banking in Florida," 77; Dewey, *State Banking,* 168, 179–80; Kroos and Blyn, *History of Financial Intermediaries,* 29.

58. J. E. Dovell, *History of Banking in Florida, 1828–1954* (Orlando: Florida Bankers Association, 1955), 25–26.

59. Thomas, "History of Banking in Florida," 87.

60. Dovell, *History of Banking in Florida*, 19.

61. *Florida House Journal*, 1842, 266.

62. House Document 226, 29th Cong., 1st sess., 783. The previous year the bank's ratio of specie to notes had been one thirty-seventh. See Thomas, "History of Banking in Florida," 94.

63. Thomas, "History of Banking in Florida," 110.

64. Apalachicola *Commercial Advertiser*, 1 January 1844, p. 4.

65. Paul B. Trescott, *Financing American Enterprise: The Story of Commercial Banking* (New York: Harper and Row, 1963), 31.

66. Kroos and Blyn, *History of Financial Intermediaries*, 79.

67. Thomas, "History of Banking in Florida," Table I. The territory of Florida chartered three other banks for Apalachicola, but Congress disallowed them.

68. Marckhoff, "Development of Currency and Banking," 123.

69. House Document 226, 29th Cong., 1st sess., 729.

70. Thomas, "History of Banking in Florida," Table III.

71. Harry P. Owens, "Apalachicola Before 1861" (Ph.D. diss., Florida State University, 1966), 215–16.

72. Dovell, *History of Banking in Florida*, 42.

73. These men were: Hiram W. Brooks, agent for the Mechanics Bank of Augusta, Georgia; William G. Porter, agent for the Augusta Insurance and Banking Company; Nathaniel J. Deblois, agent of the Marine and Fire Insurance Company; Daniel K. Dodge, agent of the Bank of Georgetown; Thomas L. Mitchel, agent for the Union Bank of South Carolina; John C. Maclay, agent of the Bank of the State of Georgia; and Samuel Cassin, Bank of Charleston. All were cotton commission merchants. See *Southern Business Directory and General Commercial Advertiser*, vol. 1 (Charleston: Walker and James, 1854), 135.

74. Austin and Long to Farish Carter, 31 October 1850, Carter Papers.

75. Trescott, *Financing American Enterprise*, 35.

76. Apalachicola *Commercial Advertiser*, 8 January 1844, p. 3.

77. Bank of Columbus business card in DeVotie Scrapbook, Manuscript Department, William R. Perkins Library, Duke University. The agencies were located in Bainbridge, Fort Gaines, Blakely, Lumpkin, Cuthbert, and Talbotton, Georgia; Open Pond, and Abbeville, Alabama; and Marianna, Tallahassee, and Apalachicola, Florida.

78. Mobile also had a shallow harbor, which forced cotton shippers to lighter their cargo to the ships that could not come to the city docks, but this inconvenience did not prevent the port from thriving.

79. Dugas to William Dearing, 25 January 1845, L. F. E. Dugas Letter-

book, Southern Historical Collection, University of North Carolina, Chapel Hill.

80. Kroos and Blyn, *History of Financial Intermediaries*, 80.

81. Harold F. Williamson, "Money and Commercial Banking, 1789–1861," in *The Growth of the American Economy: An Introduction to the Economic History of the United States*, ed. Harold F. Williamson (New York: Prentice-Hall, 1944), 268.

82. Ratner, Soltow, and Sylla, *Evolution of the American Economy*, 167.

83. *Columbus Enquirer*, 26 April 1843, p. 3.

84. Ibid., 30 October 1844, p. 3, 8 December 1846, p. 3, 9 November 1847, p. 3; Columbus *Times*, 25 April 1848, p. 3; House Executive Document 68, 31st Cong., 1st sess., 244–45.

85. *Columbus Enquirer*, 2 June 1850, p. 3; Albany *Patriot*, 8 November 1850, p. 3.

86. John H. Martin, comp., *Columbus, Geo., From Its Selection as a 'Trading Town' in 1827 to its Partial Destruction by Wilson's Raid in 1865* (Columbus: Thomas Gilbert Pub., 1874), Part II, 56; Daniel G. Cassidy, *The Illustrated History of Florida Paper Money* (Jacksonville, Fla.: Mendelson Printing and Office Supply Co., 1980), 29.

87. It had been illegal to secure a loan with cotton ever since 1840. Dewey, *State Banking*, 48.

88. *Columbus Enquirer*, 30 October 1844, p. 3, 8 December 1846, p. 3, 9 November 1847, p. 3; *Columbus Times*, 25 April 1848, p. 3; *Columbus Enquirer*, 25 April 1848, p. 3, 2 June 1850, p. 3.

89. Paris Tillinghast to Samuel Tillinghast, 17 July 1854, Tillinghast Papers.

90. *Southern Business Directory*, 270, 276.

91. Columbus *Times* and *Columbus Enquirer*, passim; *Southern Business Directory*, 270, 276, listed six: John D. Carter, agent, Augusta Insurance and Banking Company; R. B. Murdock, agent, Bank of Charleston; Schley and Johnson, agents, Bank of Savannah; H. H. Epping, agent, Bank of Brunswick and Union Bank of Georgia; John Munn, agent for Protection Insurance Co., North Carolina Mutual Insurance Co., Sun Mutual Insurance Co., and others; and Paul J. Semmes, agent, Bank of State of Georgia. There were five agencies there in 1857. See *Bankers Magazine*, vol. 6, New Series (June 1857): 994.

92. Bank of Brunswick statements published in *Columbus Enquirer*, 15 October 1845, p. 3, 2 November 1847, p. 3; Columbus *Times*, 18 April 1848, p. 3; *Columbus Enquirer*, 1 May 1849, p. 3.

93. Columbus *Times*, 11 March 1846, p. 2.

94. *Columbus Enquirer*, 13 March 1855, p. 2, 22 January 1850, p. 2.

95. Paris Tillinghast to Samuel Tillinghast, 20 February 1855, Tillinghast Papers.

96. Ibid., 17 July 1854.

97. *Columbus Enquirer*, 16 February 1842, p. 1.

98. *Bankers Magazine*, vol. 10, New Series (July 1860): 53–54. Bainbridge had one in 1861. See ibid. (June 1861): 954–55.

99. Apalachicola *Commercial Advertiser*, 26 February 1844, p. 1.

100. Columbus *Times*, 18 March 1841, p. 2.

101. E. J. Donnell charts the price of cotton over the years in *Chronological and Statistical History of Cotton*, 252–344.

102. Heath, *Constructive Liberalism*, 223.

103. Albany *Patriot*, 6 March 1856. An agency of the Bank of Charleston, South Carolina, was there in 1855. Ibid., 1 November 1855, p. 3.

104. Ibid., 12 April 1850, p. 2, 10 May 1850, p. 2.

105. Apalachicola *Commercial Advertiser*, 27 April 1844, p. 2; *Columbus Enquirer*, 13 October 1858, p. 2.

106. Albany *Patriot*, 26 March 1857, p. 2, 1 May 1858, p. 2.

107. Chester W. Wright, *Economic History of the United States* (New York: McGraw-Hill, 1941), 476–77; Margaret Myers, *A Financial History of the United States* (New York: Columbia University Press, 1970), 126–27.

108. Heath, *Constructive Liberalism*, 225.

109. Albany *Patriot*, 22 October 1857, p. 2.

110. *Columbus Enquirer*, 10 December 1857, p. 2.

111. James Slade to Fannie Roulhac, 4 November 1857, Ruffin-Roulhac-Hamilton Family Papers, Southern Historical Collection, University of North Carolina, Chapel Hill.

112. This was the second Bank of Columbus. The first one had been organized in 1829, began operation in 1832, and succumbed during the depression in 1842. See John H. Martin, *Columbus, Geo.*, 19, 36. Paris Tillinghast to Samuel Tillinghast, 7 April 1842, Tillinghast Papers.

113. At least ten of the stockholders were Apalachicola commission merchants. Young was by far the largest stockholder, having 415 shares of a total 2,500. See Albany *Patriot*, 23 April 1857, p. 2.

114. *Columbus Enquirer*, 10 July 1858, p. 3.

115. Paris Tillinghast to Samuel Tillinghast, 26 February 1860, Tillinghast Papers.

## 5. Financing the Cotton Trade

1. David L. Cohn, *The Life and Times of King Cotton* (New York: Oxford University Press, 1956), 113.

2. Dugas to Messrs. Pillot and Le Barbier, 13 May 1845, and Dugas to Victor Ponté, 17 May 1845, in Dugas Family Papers, Manuscript Department, William R. Perkins Library, Duke University.

3. Farmers often got advances in the form of cash for their cotton from either a warehouse owner, a country storekeeper, or an agent of a coastal factor. See Harold D. Woodman, *King Cotton and His Retainers: Financing and Marketing the Cotton Crop of the South, 1800–1925* (Lexington: University of Kentucky Press, 1968), 34.

4. T. S. Miller, Sr., *The American Cotton System Historically Treated Showing Operations of the Cotton Exchanges* (Austin: Austin Printing Co., 1909), 242.

5. Pillot and Le Barbier *v.* Joseph B. Brooks, Pleadings and related papers, Dugas Family Papers, Manuscript Department, William R. Perkins Library, Duke University.

6. Miller, *The American Cotton System*, 201.

7. Pillot and Le Barbier *v.* Joseph B. Brooks, Dugas Family Papers, Manuscript Department, William R. Perkins Library, Duke University.

8. Edwin Perkins, *Financing Anglo-American Trade: The House of Brown, 1800–1880* (Cambridge, Mass., and London: Harvard University Press, 1975), 8–9.

9. Ibid., 9.

10. William A. Kain to Farish Carter, 12 April 1855, Farish Carter Papers, Southern Historical Collection, University of North Carolina, Chapel Hill.

11. *Columbus Enquirer,* 16 January 1855, p. 2, and 21 January 1858, p. 2.

12. Ibid., 21 January 1858, p. 2.

13. George D. Green, *Finance and Economic Development in the Old South: Louisiana Banking, 1804–1861* (Stanford: Stanford University Press, 1972), 74.

14. Ibid., 76.

15. Austin and Long to Farish Carter, 6 December 1851, Farish Carter Papers.

16. T. H. Austin and Co. Entry, R. G. Dun Collection, Florida Vol. 3:218, Baker Library, Harvard University Graduate School of Business Administration, Harvard University.

17. Margaret G. Myers, *Origins and Development*, Vol. 1 of *The New York Money Market* (New York: Columbia University Press, 1931), 49–52.

18. Two examples are found in Austin Long and Company to Samuel Carter, 9 April 1853, Farish Carter Papers, Southern Historical Collection, University of North Carolina, Chapel Hill; and John Horry Dent Papers, 3:41–42, Historic Chattahoochee Commission, Eufaula, Alabama.

19. William G. Porter and Company to David Barrow, 3 January 1855, Barrow Papers.

20. D. K. Dodge to Abraham Bell and Son, 10 March 1846, in Box 37, Manuscripts, P. K. Yonge Library, University of Florida, Gainesville.

21. Brown Brothers and Company, Ledger Accounts, passim, Manuscript Division, New York Public Library.

22. L. F. E. Dugas Letterbook, passim, Southern Historical Collection, University of North Carolina, Chapel Hill; and Dugas Family Papers, passim, Manuscript Department, William R. Perkins Library, Duke University.

23. Dugas to Messrs. Poirier Freres, 21 January 1845, Dugas Papers, Southern Historical Collection, University of North Carolina, Chapel Hill.

24. Ibid.

25. Nourse, Brooks and Company, to Phelps-Dodge and Company, 6 May 1840, Phelps-Dodge Papers, Box 4—Letters, Manuscript Division, New York Public Library.

26. See Brown Brothers and Company Records, passim.

27. Brown Brothers and Company, Ledger Accounts, passim. This commission was the standard offered to all the Brown agents in the South. See Perkins, *Financing Anglo-American Trade*, 97, 109.

28. *Bankers Magazine*, 10 (January 1861): 695–96, 699. Florida's legal interest rate was 8 percent from 1844 to 1855, but 6 percent thereafter. See Apalachicola *Commercial Advertiser*, 22 June 1844, p. 1.

29. See 1854 Ellison account in Chandler C. Yonge Papers, P. K. Yonge Library, University of Florida, Gainesville.

30. Woodman, *King Cotton and His Retainers*, 53; Fred Mitchell Jones, *Middlemen in the Domestic Trade of the United States, 1800–1860* (1937; reprint, New York: Johnson Reprint Corp., 1968), 23.

31. Hines Holt to Farish Carter, 18 May 1843, Farish Carter Papers.

32. See entry of 14 August 1838 in Nelson Tift Diary, Southern Historical Collection, University of North Carolina, Chapel Hill.

33. Nourse, Brooks and Company to Phelps-Dodge and Company, 6 May 1840, Phelps-Dodge Papers.

34. Apalachicola *Commercial Advertiser,* 9 January 1847, p. 3.

35. *Apalachicolian,* 26 December 1840, p. 3.

36. Apalachicola *Commercial Advertiser,* 9 November 1844, p. 3. Being able to sell exchange in any amount indicated Mitchel was drawing fresh drafts on his correspondents for the sole purpose of profiting from selling exchange rather than by selling the second-hand bills that he accumulated through the course of dealing in cotton at whatever amounts they happened to be in.

37. See John Horry Dent Papers, 2:215, 218, 221.

38. George S. Hawkins to Farish Center, 30 December 1843, Farish Carter Papers.

39. Walter B. Smith and Arthur H. Cole, *Fluctuations in American Business, 1790–1860* (Cambridge: Harvard University Press, 1935), 127.

# 6. Cotton Men

1. Apalachicola *Commercial Advertiser,* 30 September 1844, p. 2.

2. Quoted in Niles Schuh, ed., "Apalachicola in 1838–1840: Letters from a Young Cotton Warehouse Clerk," *Florida Historical Quarterly* 68, no. 3 (January 1990), 318.

3. Ibid., 317.

4. Ibid., 316.

5. Ibid., 317.

6. Ibid.

7. Nicholas A. Long to Farish Carter, 13 March 1853, Farish Carter Papers, Southern Historical Collection, University of North Carolina, Chapel Hill.

8. David L. Cohn, *The Life and Times of King Cotton* (New York: Oxford University Press, 1956), 114; James Curtis Ballagh, ed., *Southern Economic History* (Richmond, Va.: Southern Historical Publication Society, 1909), 403.

9. Alexander A. Allen to George Washington Allen, 24 December 1849, George W. Allen Papers, Southern Historical Collection.

10. D. K. Dodge to Abraham Bell and Son, 10 March 1846, in Box 37, Manuscripts, P. K. Yonge Library, University of Florida, Gainesville.

11. John Horry Dent Papers, passim, Historic Chattahoochee Commission, Eufaula.

12. *Columbus Enquirer,* 10 October 1854, p. 3, and 24 October 1854, p. 2.

13. See Harold D. Woodman, *King Cotton and His Retainers: Financing*

*and Marketing the Cotton Crop of the South, 1800–1925* (Lexington: University of Kentucky Press, 1968), 67–68.

14. John Horry Dent Papers, passim; Anne Kendrick Walker, *Backtracking in Barbour County* (Richmond, Va.: Dietz Press, 1941), 141.

15. *Columbus Enquirer*, 2 June 1842, p. 2.

16. Apalachicola *Commercial Advertiser*, 12 April 1843, quoted in Rose Gibbons Lovett, "Excerpts and Articles Relating to Apalachicola and Area," 13–14, Lovett Family Papers, Florida State Archives, Tallahassee.

17. Apalachicola *Watchman of the Gulf*, 12 August 1843, p. 4.

18. Harry P. Owens, "Apalachicola Before 1861" (Ph.D. diss., Florida State University, 1966), 244.

19. *Columbus Enquirer*, 30 July 1845, p. 3.

20. Ibid., 10 September 1845, p. 1.

21. Ibid.

22. H. S. Smith and Company advertisement in ibid.

23. Business card in James H. DeVotie Scrapbook, Manuscript Department, William R. Perkins Library, Duke University.

24. *Columbus Enquirer*, 16 August 1843, p. 3.

25. Ibid.; Columbus *Times*, 9 December 1841, p. 3.

26. Columbus *Times*, 9 September 1841, p. 3, and 9 September 1846, p. 4.

27. Muscogee Superior Court Records, Books A–G (1840–1858), Georgia State Archives, Atlanta.

28. Redd and Johnson Day Book, vol. 5 of Redd and Johnson Papers, Southern Historical Collection.

29. Apalachicola *Commercial Advertiser*, 30 November 1844, p. 1.

30. Raphael J. Moses Autobiography, Southern Historical Collection; U.S. Congress, *Seventh Census, 1850*, population schedule, Franklin County, Florida.

31. Nancy Telfair, *A History of Columbus, Georgia, 1828–1928* (Columbus: Historical Publishing Co., 1929), n.p.

32. Dugas to Rossignol, 28 February 1845, L. F. E. Dugas Letterbook, Southern Historical Collection.

33. Albany *Patriot*, 1 November 1855, p. 3.

34. Etta Blanchard Worsley, *Columbus on the Chattahoochee* (Columbus: Columbus Office Supply Co., 1951), 223–24; Columbus *Times*, 28 October 1846, p. 3; Albany *Patriot*, 5 January 1855, p. 3, and 17 September 1857, p. 3.

35. Daniel J. Day to Jeremiah Day, 17 June 1850, Niles Schuh private collection, Panama City, Florida.

36. These firms were Howard and Rutherford, Farrior and McCully, and the associates known as Nourse, Stone and Company of Apalachicola and B. F. Nourse and Company of New Orleans. *Columbus Enquirer,* 10 September 1845, p. 1; Marianna *Florida Whig,* 15 July 1846, p. 3; Columbus *Times,* 4 January 1848, p. 4.

37. Of the ten merchants who never had a partner, only six men had any longevity in business alone. They were: Nathaniel J. Deblois, Barnard Ellis, Benjamin S. Hawley, Thomas L. Mitchel, Banjamin Salter, and Isaac M. Wright.

38. *Columbus Enquirer,* 8 September 1841, p. 1.

39. Ibid., 4 October 1843, p. 3, and 6 September 1843, p. 3.

40. Ibid., 9 October 1844, p. 1.

41. Ibid., 5 October 1852, p. 3.

42. Ibid., 21 June 1853, p. 3.

43. Apalachicola *Commercial Advertiser,* 16 September 1840, p. 4, and 30 November 1844, p. 1; *Columbus Enquirer,* 24 November 1846, p. 1.

44. Apalachicola *Commercial Advertiser,* 1 January 1844, p. 1, and 11 April 1846, p. 3.

45. Entry of 2 March 1838, Nelson Tift Diary, Southern Historical Collection.

46. Entry of 6 September 1840, in ibid.

47. Entry of 26 January 1842, in ibid.

48. Entry of 15 August 1842, in ibid.

49. Entry of 23 June 1843, in ibid.

50. Thomas L. Mitchel Entry, R. G. Dun Collection, Florida Vol. 3:203, Baker Library, Harvard Graduate School of Business Administration, Harvard University.

51. Fletcher M. Green, *The Role of the Yankee in the Old South* (Athens: University of Georgia Press, 1972), 130; William W. Chenault and Robert C. Reinders, "The Northern-born Community of New Orleans in the 1850s," *Journal of American History* 51, no. 2 (September 1964): 233.

52. Harriet E. Amos, "'Birds of Passage' in a Cotton Port: Northerners and Foreigners among the Urban Leaders of Mobile, 1820–1860," in *Class, Conflict, and Consensus: Antebellum Southern Community Studies,* ed. Orville Vernon Burton and Robert C. McMath, Jr. (Westport, Conn.: Greenwood Press, 1982), 242.

53. Ibid., 254.

54. The studies of New Orleans, Mobile, and Apalachicola cannot be directly compared since the New Orleans figures relate to total population,

while the Mobile study centered on civic leaders, many of whom were also in commerce. Apalachicola statistics refer to commercial proprietors only, regardless of their standing in the community.

55. Of the 101 known merchants who were proprietors of an Apalachicola cotton factorage business, there is information on the nativity of only one-half of them. Most notherners were from Connecticut and New York. Six percent were foreign-born. See U.S. Congress, *Seventh Census, 1850*, and U.S. Congress, *Eighth Census, 1860*, Franklin County, Florida; R. G. Dun Collection, passim.

56. Cora Mitchel, *Reminiscences of the Civil War* (Providence, R.I.: Snow and Farnham Co., [1916]), 4.

57. Charles Rogers to Caleb Hopkins, 30 November 1838, Box 37, Manuscripts, P. K. Yonge Library, University of Florida.

58. Apalachicola *Commercial Advertiser,* 13 June 1846, p. 2.

59. T. J. Cantrell to Mrs. C. G. Falconar, 25 July 1840, Falconar Papers, MS. 345.1, Maryland Historical Society Library, Baltimore.

60. Apalachicola *Commercial Advertiser,* 11 May, 18 May, 1 June, 22 June, 29 June 1844, all on p. 3.

61. Lovett, "Excerpts and Articles," 9.

62. Sophy Cantrell to Mrs. Sarah Cantrell, 22 August 1840, Falconar Papers.

63. Apalachicola *Commercial Advertiser,* 26 August 1843, quoted in Lovett, "Excerpts and Articles," 18.

64. Apalachicola *Commercial Advertiser,* 13 June 1846, p. 2.

65. Ibid., 4 November 1847, p. 2.

66. T. J. Cantrell to Mrs. Sarah Cantrell, 6 March 1838, Falconar Papers.

67. T. J. Cantrell to Mrs. Sarah Cantrell, 8 November 1836, Falconar Papers.

68. Apalachicola *Commercial Advertiser,* 2 May 1846, p. 3.

69. Mitchel, *Reminiscences of the Civil War,* 4.

70. The census of 1860 was taken in June after the business season was over and is therefore grossly lacking in information about the mostly itinerant population.

71. Harriet E. Amos, *Cotton City: Urban Development in Antebellum Mobile* (Tuscaloosa: University of Alabama Press, 1985), 61.

72. Rhea Cumming Otto, "1850 Census of Geo. (Muscogee County)," N.p., 1977, passim.

73. R. G. Dun Collection, passim.

74. Trinity Episcopal Church Records, Trinity Church, Apalachicola.

75. For photographs of the houses of some of Columbus's commission merchants, see Worsley, *Columbus on the Chattahoochee,* 223–24, 225–27; Mollie Mealing, *Century Old Houses of Columbus, Georgia and Vicinity* (Columbus: Columbus Office Supply Co., 1971), no. 34; F. Clason Kyle, *Images: A Pictorial History of Columbus, Georgia* (Norfolk, Va.: Donning Co., 1986), 29.

76. Robert Royal Russel, *Economic Aspects of Southern Sectionalism, 1840–1861* (Urbana: University of Illinois, 1924), 100.

77. Ibid.

## 7. The End of an Era

1. Carter Goodrich, et al., *Canals and American Economic Development* (New York: Columbia University Press, 1961), 7.

2. Joe Knetsch, "The Canal Era in West Florida: 1821–1845," *Gulf Coast Historical Review* 7, no. 1 (Fall 1991): 50; and Joe Knetsch, "Canal Fever in North Florida," *Apalachee* 10 (1991): 51–52.

3. U.S. Congress, *Senate Journal,* Document 199, 24th Cong., 1st sess., 6.

4. Rose Gibbons Lovett, "The Trilogy of the Tri-Rivers: Apalachicola, Chattahoochee, and Flint Rivers" (Typescript in Lovett Family Papers, Florida State Archives, Tallahassee), 23–42.

5. Harry P. Owens, "Sail and Steam Vessels Serving the Apalachicola-Chattahoochee Valley," *Alabama Review* (July 1968): 201.

6. Albany *Patriot,* 3 August 1849, p. 3.

7. Ibid., 15 June 1849, p. 2.

8. *Columbus Enquirer,* 11 October 1843, p. 3, and 22 November 1843, p. 3; Cecil W. McDonald, "The Economic History of Columbus, Georgia to the Civil War" (Master's thesis, Auburn University, 1940), 48.

9. *Columbus Enquirer,* 11 January 1860, reprinted in Thomas Joseph Peddy, comp., "Chattahoochee River Steamboats from Columbus, Georgia Newspapers," vol. 1 (Handbound typescript), 73.

10. *Commercial Advertiser,* 22 January 1844, p. 3.

11. Apalachicola *Courier,* 15 October 1839, p. 2.

12. John H. Martin, comp., *Columbus Geo., From Its Selection as a 'Trading Town' in 1827 to its Partial Destruction by Wilson's Raid in 1865,* Part I (Columbus: Thomas Gilbert Pub., 1874; reprint, N.p.: Georgia Genealogical Reprints, 1972), p. 68.

13. Albany *Patriot,* 8 June 1849, p. 2.

14. Martin, *Columbus, Geo.*, II:164.

15. *Columbus Enquirer*, 22 February 1853, p. 2.

16. Owens, "Sail and Steam Vessels," 207.

17. *Merchants' Magazine* 2:84 and 24:628.

18. "Florida in 1845," a map reprinted in Dorothy Dodd, *Florida Becomes a State* (Tallahassee: Record Press, 1945), n.p.

19. Albert Burton Moore, *History of Alabama* (University, Ala.: Alabama Book Store, 1934), 294.

20. Ibid.

21. Columbus *Times and Sentinel*, 7 February 1854, p. 2.

22. George Rogers Taylor, *The Transportation Revolution, 1815–1860*, vol. 4 of *The Economic History of the United States* (New York: Harper and Row, 1951), 71. The steamboat *Champion* set a new speed record for the round trip between Apalachicola and Columbus in 1844, averaging just over ten miles per hour. See *Commercial Advertiser*, 12 February 1844, p. 2.

23. Ulrich Bonnell Phillips, *A History of Transportation in the Eastern Cotton Belt to 1860* (New York: Columbia University Press, 1908; reprint, New York: Octagon Books, 1968), 17; Milton Sydney Heath, *Constructive Liberalism: The Role of the State in Economic Development in Georgia to 1860* (Cambridge: Harvard University Press, 1954), 278–79.

24. Phillips, *History of Transportation*, 17–18.

25. Ibid., 18.

26. Heath, *Constructive Liberalism*, 279.

27. Ibid.

28. Columbus *Times*, 4 November 1846, p. 2.

29. Heath, *Constructive Liberalism*, 279–80.

30. *Columbus Enquirer*, 14 May 1845, p. 2.

31. Columbus *Times*, 1 February 1848, p. 2.

32. Heath, *Constructive Liberalism*, 280.

33. *Columbus Enquirer*, 7 May 1845, p. 2; Columbus *Times*, 22 February 1848, p. 2.

34. Columbus *Times*, 9 December 1851, p. 1.

35. Heath, *Constructive Liberalism*, 253.

36. Columbus *Times*, 7 October 1851, p. 1.

37. Albany *Patriot*, 7 June, 28 June, and 12 July 1850, all on p. 2.

38. Ibid., 12 April 1850, p. 1.

39. *Spirit of the South*, 1853, quoted in Mattie Thomas Thompson, *History of Barbour County* (Eufaula: N.p., 1939), 32.

40. Ibid., 30–31; Heath, *Constructive Liberalism*, 252–53.

41. Heath, *Constructive Liberalism*, 253.
42. *Columbus Enquirer*, 21 September 1852, p. 2.
43. Ibid., 24 May 1853, p. 2.
44. Ibid.
45. Columbus *Times*, 8 February 1848, p. 2.
46. *Columbus Enquirer*, 1851–53, passim.
47. Albany *Patriot*, 8 December 1854; Columbus *Times*, 22 February 1848, p. 2.
48. Clay County Library, *The History of Clay County* ([Fort Gaines, Ga.]: N.p., 1976), 8.
49. Columbus *Times and Sentinel*, 17 January 1854, p. 2.
50. *Columbus Enquirer*, 27 February 1855, p. 2.
51. Ibid., 17 March 1857, p. 2.
52. T. D. Clark, "The Montgomery and West Point Railroad Company," *Georgia Historical Quarterly* 17, no. 1 (March 1933): 297.
53. Harriet E. Amos, *Cotton City: Urban Development in Antebellum Mobile* (Tuscaloosa: University of Alabama Press, 1985), 204–05.
54. Ibid., 205.
55. *Columbus Enquirer*, 19 October 1858, p. 3.
56. Ibid., 23 October 1858, p. 3.
57. Ibid., 25 March 1858, p. 3.
58. Harry P. Owens, "Apalachicola Before 1861" (Ph.D. diss., Florida State University, 1966), 248.
59. Ibid., 249.
60. Reprinted in Columbus *Enquirer*, 19 April 1853, p. 2.
61. *Columbus Enquirer*, 27 February and 27 March 1855, both on p. 2.
62. Reprinted in *Columbus Enquirer*, 25 October 1853, p. 2.
63. Paris Tillinghast to Samuel Tillinghast, 20 November 1853, Tillinghast Papers, Manuscript Department, William R. Perkins Library, Duke University, Durham, North Carolina.
64. *Columbus Enquirer*, 18 November 1856, reprinted in Peddy, "Chattahoochee River Steamboats," 59.
65. Apalachicola *Commercial Advertiser*, 2 May 1846, p. 3.
66. Ibid., 9 December 1848, p. 2.
67. Ibid., 9 March 1848, p. 2.
68. Ibid.
69. Ibid., 9 March and 9 December 1848; Albany *Patriot*, 31 May 1850, all on p. 2.
70. Albany *Patriot*, 31 May 1850, p. 2.

71. Ibid., 31 May 1850, and 18 April 1851; *Commercial Advertiser*, 12 February 1844, all on p. 2. A new boat and barge line from Albany to Apalachicola was instituted in 1855 by Albany businessmen, but there is no record of its results. See Albany *Patriot*, 1 November 1855, p. 3. The Southwestern Railroad reached Albany two years later.

72. Albany *Patriot*, 1 April 1858, p. 2.

73. Ibid., 27 January 1849, and 22 December 1854, both on p. 2.

74. See W. H. Long to Farish Carter, 8 July 1853, Farish Carter Papers, Southern Historical Collection, University of North Carolina.

75. *Columbus Enquirer*, 23 June 1857, p. 2; *Florida House Journal*, 10th sess., 1860, 17.

76. *Florida House Journal*, 10th sess., 1860, 14.

77. Reprinted in the *Columbus Enquirer*, 21 February 1860, and found in Peddy, "Chattahoochee River Steamboats," 74.

78. Ibid.

79. Albany *Patriot*, 28 May 1857, p. 2; *Columbus Enquirer*, 24 June 1858, p. 2.

80. See Table 7-3 for Savannah receipts from 1842 to 1859.

81. *Columbus Enquirer*, 9 June 1857, p. 2.

82. Ibid.

83. Ibid., 14 November 1854, p. 2.

84. Ibid.

85. Ibid.; Albany *Patriot*, 11 March 1858, p. 2.

86. Hines Holt to Farish Carter, 27 December 1855, Farish Carter Papers.

87. Albany *Patriot*, 25 February 1858, p. 2.

88. *Columbus Enquirer*, 5 February 1856, p. 2; Martin, *Columbus, Geo.*, II:120.

89. James L. Watkins, *King Cotton: A Historical and Statistical Review, 1790–1908* (1908; reprint, New York: Negro Universities Press, 1969), 32.

90. Columbus *Times and Sentinel*, passim.

91. Phillips, *History of Transportation*, 20.

92. Sidney Ratner, James H. Soltow, and Richard Sylla, *The Evolution of the American Economy: Growth, Welfare, and Decision Making* (New York: Basic Books, 1979), 123.

93. Lacy K. Ford, "Rednecks and Merchants: Economic Tensions in the South Carolina Upcountry, 1865–1900," *Journal of American History* 71 (September 1984): 307.

94. Phillips, *History of Transportation*, 20.

# *Bibliography*

## Primary Sources

### U.S. Documents

U.S. Congress *Sixth Census, 1840.* Washington, D.C.: Blair and Rives, 1841.

———. *Seventh Census, 1850.* Washington, D.C.: Robert Armstrong, 1853.

———. *Seventh Census, 1850.* Original Schedules. Franklin, Jackson, [etc.] Counties, Florida. [same for Alabama and Georgia].

———. *Eighth Census, 1860.* Washington, D.C.: U.S. Government Printing Office, 1864.

———. House of Representatives. *Condition of the State Banks.* Document no. 111. 26th Cong., 2nd sess., 1840.

———. *Condition of the State Banks.* Document no. 226. 29th Cong., 1st sess., 1845.

———. *Condition of the State Banks.* Executive Document no. 68. 31st Cong., 1st sess., 1849.

———. *Condition of the State Banks.* Executive Document no. 107. 35th Cong., 1st sess., 1857.

———. *Condition of the State Banks.* Executive Document no. 112. 35th Cong., 2nd sess., 1859.

———. Senate. *Report of Israel D. Andrews . . . on the Trade and Com-*

merce of the British North American Colonies. . . . Senate Executive
Document No. 112. 32nd Cong., 1st sess., 1853.
———. *Senate Journal.* Document no. 199. 24th Cong., 1st sess., 1836.


## State Documents

*Acts of the General Assembly of the State of Georgia, 1835.* Milledgeville:
John A. Cuthbert, 1836.
*Acts of the General Assembly of the State of Georgia, 1851–52.* Macon:
Samuel J. Ray, State Printer, 1852.
Cobb, T. R. R., reporter. *Reports of Cases in Law and Equity Argued and
Determined in the Supreme Court of the State of Georgia.* Vol. 12.
Athens, Ga.: Christy and Kelsea, 1853.
Florida. *Journal of the Florida Legislative Council.* 1840.
———. *House Journal.* 1841.
———. *Senate Journal.* 1841.
———. *House Journal.* 1842.
———. *House Journal.* 1860.


## Books

*Bicknell's Counterfeit Detector and Bank Note List.* Vol. 8, no. 9 (1 Sep-
tember 1840). Vol. 13, nos. 5 and 6 (1 and 15 March 1844).
Buckingham, James S. *The Slave States of America.* 2 vols. London: Fisher,
Son and Co., 1842.
[Campbell, John P.] *The Southern Business Directory and General Com-
mercial Advertiser.* Vol. 1. Charleston: Steam Power Press of Walker and
James, 1854.
*Columbus City Directory, 1859–1860.* Columbus: Sun Book and Job Print-
ing Office, 1859.
Entz, John F. *Exchange and the Cotton Trade between England and the
United States.* New York: E. B. Clayton, 1840.
Featherstonhaugh, George W. *Excursion Through the Slave States.* New
York: Harper and Brothers, 1844.
Foster, Lillian. *Wayside Glimpses, North and South.* N.p.: Rudd and
Carleton, 1860. Reprint. New York: Negro Universities Press, 1969.

*Foster's Late Days New York Counterfeit Recorder and Bank Note Table.* New York: N.p., 1850.

Kettell, Thomas Prentice. *Southern Wealth and Northern Profits.* New York: George W. and John A. Wood, 1860.

McCulloch, J. R. *A Dictionary, Practical, Theoretical, and Historical, of Commerce and Commercial Navigation.* London: A. Spotteswoode, 1839.

Mears and Co., comp. *The Columbus Directory for 1859–60 Containing the Names of the Inhabitants, A Business Directory, Street Directory, and an Appendix.* Columbus: Sun Book and Job Printing Office, 1859.

Mitchel, Cora. *Reminiscences of the Civil War.* Providence, R.I.: Snow and Farnham Co., [1916].

Olmsted, Frederick Law. *The Cotton Kingdom. A Traveller's Observations on Cotton and Slavery in the American Slave States.* Edited by Arthur Schlesinger. New York: Alfred A. Knopf, 1953.

*Southern Business Directory and General Commercial Advertiser.* Vol. 1. Charleston: Walker and James, 1854.

Thompson, John, comp. *The Autographical Counterfeit Detector, Companion to the Bank Note and Commercial Reporter . . . Containing Fac-Simile Signatures of the President and Cashier of Nearly Every Bank in the United States.* 5th ed. New York: John Thompson, 1853.

Walker, Amasa. *The Nature and Uses of Money and Mixed Currency with a History of the Wickaboag Bank.* Boston: Crosby, Nichols and Co., 1857.

White, George. *Statistics of the State of Georgia.* Savannah: W. Thorne Williams, 1849. Reprint. Spartanburg, S.C.: Reprint Co., 1972.

## Manuscripts

Abercrombie, Anderson. Accounts. Southern Historical Collection. University of North Carolina. Chapel Hill.

Allen, George W. Papers. Southern Historical Collection. University of North Carolina. Chapel Hill.

Apalachicola *Commercial Advertiser* Prices Current. Box 37. P. K. Yonge Library of Florida History. University of Florida. Gainesville.

Baker, Eleanor J. W. Papers. Manuscript Department. William R. Perkins Library. Duke University. Durham, North Carolina.

Banks, John. Invoice. Box 7. P. K. Yonge Library of Florida History. University of Florida. Gainesville.

Banks Family. Papers. Manuscript Division. University of Georgia Library. Athens.

Barbour, John N. Papers. Manuscript Department. William R. Perkins Library. Duke University. Durham, North Carolina.

Barrow Papers. Southern Historical Collection. University of North Carolina. Chapel Hill.

Benning, Henry-Seaborn Jones. Papers. Columbus College Archives. Simon Schwob Memorial Library. Columbus, Georgia.

Bonner, William G. "Map of Georgia." 1847. Surveyor General Department. Georgia Archives and Records Building. Atlanta.

Bradley, William. Collection. Florida State Archives. Tallahassee.

Brown Brothers and Company. Ledger Accounts. New York Public Library.

Burrus, George J. Map. "Columbus, Ga., 1861–65." Southern Historical Collection. University of North Carolina. Chapel Hill.

Butts, J. R. "Map of Georgia." 1859. Revised in 1870 by A. G. Butts. Surveyor General Department. Georgia Archives and Records Building. Atlanta.

Carter, Farish. Papers. Southern Historical Collection. University of North Carolina. Chapel Hill.

*Cinderella*. Manifest of Passengers. Dorothy Dodd Room. Florida State Library. R. A. Gray Building. Tallahassee.

Comer, John Fletcher. Farm Journal. Southern Historical Collection. University of North Carolina. Chapel Hill.

Copeland, J. N. and Company. Invoice Book, 1851–53. Basement Vault. Barbour County Courthouse. Clayton, Alabama.

Dent, John Horry. Papers. Microfilm copy. Historic Chattahoochee Commission. Eufaula, Alabama.

"Descriptive Notes of Lands Selected." Title Section, Florida Department of Natural Resources. Marjorie Stoneman Douglas Building. Tallahassee.

DeVotie, James H. Scrapbook. Manuscript Department. William R. Perkins Library. Duke University. Durham, North Carolina.

Dodge, D. K. Letter. Box 37. P. K. Yonge Library of Florida History. University of Florida. Gainesville.

Dodge, D. K. Letter. Dorothy Dodd Room. Florida State Library. R. A. Gray Building. Tallahassee.

Dugas, L. F. E. Letterbook, 1845. Southern Historical Collection. University of North Carolina. Chapel Hill.

Dugas, L. F. E. Letterbook, 1845–47. P. K. Yonge Library of Florida History. University of Florida. Gainesville.

Dugas Family. Papers, 1845. Manuscript Department. William R. Perkins Library. Duke University. Durham, North Carolina.

Dun, R. G. and Company. Collection. Baker Library, Harvard University Graduate School of Business Administration, Harvard University.

Falconar Papers. Maryland Historical Society Library. Baltimore.

Franklin County. Papers. Florida Collection. Dorothy Dodd Room. Florida State Library. R. A. Gray Building. Tallahassee.

Gayle-Crawford Family. Papers. Southern Historical Collection. University of North Carolina. Chapel Hill.

Governors Records. Incoming Correspondence. Florida State Archives. R. A. Gray Building. Tallahassee.

Gray Family. Papers. Southern Historical Collection. University of North Carolina. Chapel Hill.

Hentz, Charles Arnold. Papers. Southern Historical Collection. University of North Carolina. Chapel Hill.

Ince, Henry Alexander. Papers. Manuscript Department. William R. Perkins Library. Duke University. Durham, North Carolina.

Kain, W. A. Letters. Box 15. P. K. Yonge Library of Florida History. University of Florida. Gainesville.

Knapp. Letter. Dorothy Dodd Room. Florida State Library. R. A. Gray Building. Tallahassee.

Lovett, Rose Gibbons. "Excerpts and Articles Relating to Apalachicola and Area." Lovett Family Papers. Florida State Archives. R. A. Gray Building. Tallahassee.

Maclay, John C. Shipping Record. Gloria Tucker Private Collection. Apalachicola, Florida.

Mallet, E. B. Letter. Box 15. P. K. Yonge Library of Florida History. University of Florida. Gainesville.

Maritime Logs and Journals. Phillips Library. Peabody Museum. Salem, Massachusetts.

Bark *Gleaner.* Journal, 4 February 1843–3 April 1844.

Bark *Kepler.* Journal, Kept by Mrs. Henry Moulton, 14 October 1859–20 March 1860.

Ship *Henry Ware.* Log, 11 March 1851–29 November 1851.

Ship *Moro Castle.* Journal, 23 February 1860–17 January 1861.

Ship *Sarah Parker.* Log, 28 January 1837–31 January 1840.

Minutes of Town Council. Book 1, 1847–57. Eufaula City Hall. Eufaula, Alabama.

Miscellaneous Southern Business Letters. Southern Historical Collection. University of North Carolina. Chapel Hill.

Moore, Thomas. Commonplace Book. Manuscript Department. William R. Perkins Library. Duke University. Durham, North Carolina.

Moses, Raphael J. Autobiography. Typescript. Southern Historical Collection. University of North Carolina. Chapel Hill.

Murdock and Wright Family. Papers. Southern Historical Collection. University of North Carolina. Chapel Hill.

Nautical Chart. E. and G. W. Blunt. "The North Coast of the Gulf of Mexico from St. Marks to Galveston." New York: Chas. Copley, 1844.

Norris, Robert. Accounts. Manuscript Department. William R. Perkins Library. Duke University. Durham, North Carolina.

Phelps-Dodge and Company. Papers, 1832–59. New York Public Library.

Philips, James J. Papers. Southern Historical Collection. University of North Carolina. Chapel Hill.

Phillips, Charles H. Family. Letters. In "Alabama-Barbour County—Letters" Folder. Carnegie Library. Eufaula, Alabama.

Prices Current Bulletins. Manuscript Department. William R. Perkins Library. Duke University. Durham, North Carolina.

Raney, David G. Tax Returns, 1859. Dorothy Dodd Room. Florida State Library. R. A. Gray Building. Tallahassee.

Redd and Johnson. Papers. Southern Historical Collection. University of North Carolina. Chapel Hill.

Redd, W. A. and Company. Account Book, 1844. In Kenneth H. Thomas Collection. Columbus College Archives. Simon Schwob Memorial Library. Columbus.

Rhind-Stokes. Papers. Manuscript Division. University of Georgia Library. Athens.

Rhodes, Mrs. Elizabeth. Diary. Typescript copy. Carnegie Library. Eufaula, Alabama.

Rogers, Charles. Papers. Box 7. P. K. Yonge Library of Florida History. University of Florida. Gainesville.

Ruffin-Roulhac-Hamilton Family. Papers. Southern Historical Collection. University of North Carolina. Chapel Hill.

Shipowner to Capt. Thomas C. Lennan. Letter. Box 37. P. K. Yonge Library of Florida History. University of Florida. Gainesville.

Shorter, James H., and B. B. Fountaine. Account Book. Columbus College Archives. Simon Schwob Memorial Library. Columbus.

Sills-Jelks. Papers. Manuscript Department. William R. Perkins Library. Duke University. Durham, North Carolina.

Smith, William Ephram. Papers. Manuscript Department. William R. Perkins Library. Duke Univesity. Durham, North Carolina.

Tappan. Letter. Dorothy Dodd Room. Florida State Library. R. A. Gray Building. Tallahassee.

Terry Family. Papers. Southern Historical Collection. University of North Carolina. Chapel Hill.

Ticknor, Francis Orray. Papers. Manuscript Department. William R. Perkins Library. Duke University, Durham, North Carolina.

Tift, Nelson. Diary. Southern Historical Collection. University of North Carolina. Chapel Hill.

Tillinghast, William Norwood. Papers. Manuscript Department. William R. Perkins Library, Duke University. Durham, North Carolina.

Trinity Episcopal Church. Records. Trinity Episcopal Church. Apalachicola, Florida.

Union Bank Bonds. Dorothy Dodd Room. Florida State Library. R. A. Gray Building. Tallahassee.

Warehouse Ledger "A." Vault. Clay County Courthouse, Fort Gaines, Georgia.

Williams, I. M. Letter. Box 37. P. K. Yonge Library of Florida History. University of Florida. Gainesville.

Wood, W. T. Letter. Dorothy Dodd Room. Florida State Library. R. A. Gray Building. Tallahassee.

Wright-Harris. Papers. Manuscript Department. William R. Perkins Library. Duke University. Durham, North Carolina.

Yonge, Chandler C. Papers. P. K. Yonge Library of Florida History. University of Florida. Gainesville.


### Newspapers

Albany *Patriot*. 1847–60.
*Apalachicolian*. 1840.
*Columbus Enquirer*. 1840–60.
Columbus *Times*. 1841–54.
Columbus *Times and Sentinel*. 1854–56.
*Commercial Advertiser* (Apalachicola). 1844–49, 185?
*Daily Commercial Register and Patriot* (Mobile). 1840–60.
*Eufaula Democrat*. 1846–49.
*Florida Whig* (Marianna). 1847–49.
*New York Herald*. 1850.
*Spirit of the South* (Eufaula). 1850–57.
*Star of the West* (Apalachicola). 1848.

## Periodicals

*American Banker.* 21 June 1899.

*Bankers' Magazine and Statistical Register.* Edited by J. Smith Homans. New York, 1846–50.

*Commercial Review of the South and West.* Edited by J. D. B. DeBow. New Orleans, 1846–50.

*DeBow's Review and Industrial Resources, Statistics, etc.* New Orleans, 1853–60.

*DeBow's Review of the Southern and Western States.* Edited by J. D. B. DeBow. New Orleans, 1850–52.

*Hunt's Merchants' Magazine.* Edited by Freeman Hunt. New York, 1850–60.

*Merchants' Magazine and Commercial Review.* Edited by Freeman Hunt. New York, 1840–50.

*Southern Cultivator.* Edited by J. W. Jones and later by James Camak and Daniel Lee. Augusta, Georgia, 1843–60.

## Secondary Sources

### Books

Albion, Robert Greenhalgh. *The Rise of New York Port, 1815–1860.* New York: Charles Scribner's Sons, 1939.

———. *Square-Riggers on Schedule: The New York Sailing Packets to England, France, and Cotton Ports.* Princeton: Princeton University Press, 1938. Reprint. Hamden, Conn.: Archon Books, 1965.

Amos, Harriet E. *Cotton City: Urban Development in Antebellum Mobile.* Tuscaloosa: University of Alabama Press, 1985.

Atherton, Lewis E. *The Southern Country Store, 1800–1860.* Baton Rouge: Louisiana State University Press, 1949. Reprint. New York: Greenwood Press, 1968.

Avery, I. W. *The History of the State of Georgia From 1850 to 1881.* New York: Brown and Derby, 1881.

Ballagh, James Curtis, ed. *Southern Economic History.* Vol. 5 of *The South in the Building of the Nation.* Richmond, Va.: Southern Historical Publication Society, 1909.

Besson, J. A. B. *History of Eufaula, Alabama: The Bluff City of the Chattahoochee.* N.p., 1875. Reprint. Spartanburg, S.C.: Reprint Co., 1976.

Bonner, James C. *A History of Georgia Agriculture, 1732–1860.* Athens: University of Georgia Press, 1964.

Brantley, William H. *Banking in Alabama, 1837–1849.* Vol. 2 of *Banking in Alabama, 1816–1860.* Birmingham, Ala.: Oxmoor Press, 1967.

Brooks, Eugene Clyde. *The Story of Cotton and the Development of the Cotton States.* New York: Rand McNally and Co., 1911.

Brown, Harry Bates. *Cotton.* 3rd edition. New York: McGraw-Hill, 1958.

Brown, John Crosby. *A Hundred Years of Merchant Banking: A History of Brown Brothers and Company, Brown, Shipley & Company and the Allied Firms.* New York: privately printed, 1909.

Bruchey, Stuart, ed. *Cotton and the Growth of the American Economy: 1790–1860.* Atlanta: Harcourt, Brace and World, 1967.

Buck, Norman Sydney. *Anglo-American Trade, 1800–1850.* N.p.: Archon Books, 1925. Reprint. New Haven: Yale University Press, 1969.

Burton, Anthony. *The Rise and Fall of King Cotton.* Rugby, England: Jolly and Barber Limeteel for British Broadcasting Corp., 1984.

Cameron, Rondo, ed. *Banking and Economic Development: Some Lessons of History.* New York: Oxford University Press, 1972.

Carothers, Neil. *Fractional Money.* New York: John Wiley and Sons, 1930. Reprint. New York: A. M. Kelly, 1967.

Cassidy, Daniel G. *The Illustrated History of Florida Paper Money.* Jacksonville, Fla.: Mendelson Printing and Office Supply Co., 1980.

Chapel, George L. *A Brief History of the Apalachicola Area.* Apalachicola: Franklin Press, n.d.

———. *Walking and Driving Tour of Historic Apalachicola.* N.p., n.d.

Clay County Library. *The History of Clay County.* [Fort Gaines, Ga.]: N.p., 1976.

Cochran, Thomas C. *Business in American Life: A History.* New York: McGraw-Hill, 1972.

Coclanis, Peter A. *The Shadow of a Dream: Economic Life and Death in the South Carolina Low Country, 1670–1920.* New York: Oxford University Press, 1989.

Cohn, David L. *The Life and Times of King Cotton.* New York: Oxford University Press, 1956.

[Colwell, Stephen.] *The Five Cotton States and New York.* [Philadelphia:] published anonymously, 1861.

Davis, Charles S. *The Cotton Kingdom in Alabama.* Montgomery: Alabama State Department of Archives and History, 1939.

Davis, Robert M. *The Southern Planter, the Factor and the Banker.* New Orleans: N.p., 1871.

Davis, William Watson. *Civil War and Reconstruction in Florida*. New York: Columbia University, 1913.

DeBow, J. D. B. *Statistical View of the United States . . . Being a Compendium of the Seventh Census*. Washington, D.C.: Beverly Tucker (Senate Printer), 1854.

Dewey, Davis R. *State Banking Before the Civil War*. Washington, D.C.: U.S. Government Printing Office, 1910.

———. *Financial History of the United States*. 9th ed. New York: Longmans, Green and Co., 1924.

Dilliston, William H. *Bank Note Reporters and Counterfeit Detectors, 1826–1866*. Numismatic Notes and Monographs, no. 114. New York: American Numismatic Society, 1949.

Dodd, Dorothy. *Apalachicola: Ante-bellum Cotton Port*. [Tallahassee]: privately published, n.d.

———. *Florida Becomes a State*. Tallahassee: Record Press, 1945.

Dodge, Bertha S. *Cotton: The Plant That Would Be King*. Austin: University of Texas Press, 1984.

Donnell, E. J. *Chronological and Statistical History of Cotton*. New York: James Sutton and Co., 1872.

Douglass, Elisha P. *The Coming of Age of American Business: Three Centuries of Enterprise, 1600–1900*. Chapel Hill: University of North Carolina Press, 1971.

Dovell, J. E. *History of Banking in Florida, 1828–1954*. Orlando: Florida Bankers Association, 1955.

Dudley, F. J. *100 Years of History of St. Luke M. E. Church, South*. Columbus: N.p., 1929.

Dunbar, Charles F. *The Theory and History of Banking*. 2nd ed. New York: G. P. Putnam's Sons, 1926.

Durant, John and Alice. *Pictorial History of American Ships on the High Seas and Inland Waters*. New York: A. S. Barnes, 1953.

Ellison, Thomas. *The Cotton Trade of Great Britain*. London: N.p., 1886. Reprint. London: Frank Cass and Co., 1968.

Escher, Franklin. *Foreign Exchange Explained*. New York: Macmillan Co., 1917.

Fairburn, William Armstrong. *Merchant Sail*. 6 vols. Center Lovell, Maine: Fairburn Marine Educational Foundation, 1945–55.

Farney, D. A. *The English Cotton Industry and the World Market, 1815–1896*. Oxford: Clarendon Press, 1979.

Florida Bureau of Land and Water Management. *The Apalachicola River and Bay System: A Florida Resource*. [Tallahassee:] F.B.L.W.M., 1977.

Fogel, Robert William, and Stanley L. Engerman, eds. *The Reinterpretation of American Economic History.* New York: Harper and Row, 1971.

Foner, Philip S. *Business and Slavery: The New York Merchants and the Irrepressible Conflict.* Chapel Hill: University of North Carolina Press, 1941.

Freeman, Harley L. *Florida Obsolete Notes and Scrip.* N.p.: Society of Paper Money Collectors, 1967.

Georgia Historical Records Survey. *Inventory of the County Archives of Georgia. No. 106 (Muscogee County).* Atlanta: Georgia Historical Records Survey, 1941.

Gibson, Jon L., ed. *Cultural Investigations in the Appalachicola and Chattahoochee River Valleys, Florida, Alabama, and Georgia: History, Archaeology and Underwater Remote Sensing.* Lafayette, La.: University of Southwest Louisiana Department of Printing Services, 1979.

Goodrich, Carter, et al. *Canals and American Economic Development.* New York: Columbia University Press, 1961.

———. *The Government and the Economy, 1783–1861.* New York: Bobbs-Merrill, 1967.

Gray, Lewis Cecil. *History of Agriculture in the Southern United States to 1860.* 2 vols. Washington, D.C.: Carnegie Institution, 1933.

Greef, Albert O. *The Commercial Paper House in the United States.* Cambridge: Harvard University Press, 1938.

Green, Fletcher M. *The Role of the Yankee in the Old South.* Athens: University of Georgia Press, 1972.

Green, George D. *Finance and Economic Development in the Old South: Louisiana Banking, 1804–1861.* Stanford: Stanford University Press, 1972.

Hamilton, Virginia Van der Veer. *Alabama: A Bicentennial History.* New York: W. W. Norton and Co., 1977.

Hammond, Bray. *Banks and Politics in America from the Revolution to the Civil War.* Princeton: Princeton University Press, 1957.

Hammond, M. B. *The Cotton Industry, An Essay in American Economic History.* New York: Macmillan Co., 1897. Reprint. New York: Johnson Reprint Corp., 1966.

Harris, Seymour E., ed. *American Economic History.* New York: McGraw-Hill, 1961.

Hatcher, George, ed. *Georgia Rivers: Articles from the Atlanta Journal and Constitution Magazine.* Athens: University of Georgia Press, 1962.

Hawk, Emory Q. *Economic History of the South.* New York: Prentice-Hall, 1934. Reprint. Westport, Conn.: Greenwood Press, 1977.

Heath, Milton Sydney. *Constructive Liberalism: The Role of the State in Economic Development in Georgia to 1860*. Cambridge: Harvard University Press, 1954.

Hepburn, A. Barton. *A History of Currency in the United States*. New York: Macmillan Co., 1903. Reprint. New York: Augustus M. Kelley, 1967.

Hidy, Ralph W. *The House of Baring in American Trade and Finance: English Merchant Bankers at Work, 1763–1861*. Cambridge: Harvard University Press, 1949.

Hobhouse, Henry. *Seeds of Change: Five plants that transformed mankind*. London: Sidgwick and Jackson, 1985.

Hummel, Ray O., Jr., ed. *Southeastern Broadsides Before 1877–A Bibliography*. Richmond: Virginia State Library, 1971.

Hunter, Louis. *Steamboats on the Western Rivers: An Economic and Technological History*. Cambridge: Harvard University Press, 1943.

Ingle, Edward. *Southern Sidelights: A Picture of Social and Economic Life in the South A Generation Before the War*. New York: Thomas Y. Crowell and Co., 1896.

Jenks, Leland Hamilton. *The Migration of British Capital to 1875*. London: Thomas Nelson and Sons, 1927. Reprint. London: Thomas Nelson and Sons, 1963.

Jones, Fred Mitchell. *Middlemen in the Domestic Trade of the United States, 1800–1860*. Urbana: University of Illinois, 1937. Reprint. New York: Johnson Reprint Corp., 1968.

Jordan, Weymouth T. *Ante-bellum Alabama: Town and Country*. Tallahassee: Florida State University, 1957. Reprint. Tuscaloosa: University of Alabama Press, 1986.

Kennedy, Joseph C. G. *Population of the United States in 1860; compiled from the Original Returns of the Eighth Census*. Washington, D.C.: U.S. Government Printing Office, 1864.

King, P. C., Jr. *Fort Gaines and Environs*. Auburn: Warren Enterprises, 1976.

Kroos, Herman E., and Martin B. Blyn. *A History of Financial Intermediaries*. New York: Random House, 1971.

Kyle, F. Clason. *Images: A Pictorial History of Columbus, Georgia*. Norfolk, Va.: Donning Co., 1986.

Lindstrom, Diane. "Domestic Trade and Regional Specialization." In Vol. 1 of *Encyclopedia of American Economic History: Studies of the Principal Movements and Ideas*. Edited by Glenn Porter. New York: Scribner's, 1980.

Lovett, Rose Gibbons. *The Lovett Family of Apalachicola, Florida and Allied Families.* Birmingham: Privately published, 1963. Microfilm copy at Florida State Archives, Tallahassee.

Lowitt, Richard. *A Merchant Prince of the Nineteenth Century: William E. Dodge.* New York: Columbia University Press, 1954.

Lupold, John. *Columbus, Georgia, 1828–1928.* Columbus: Columbus Sesquicentennial, 1978.

McGinnis, Callie B., and Sandra K. Stratford, comps. *Muscogee County, Georgia 1860 Census Index with a Short History and Bibliography by John S. Lupold.* Columbus: Yesteryear Research Associates, 1985.

Mahan, Joseph B. *Columbus: Georgia's Fall Line "Trading Town."* Northridge, Calif.: Windsor Publications, 1986.

Marriner, Sheila. *Rathbones of Liverpool, 1845–73.* Liverpool: Liverpool University Press, 1961.

Martin, John H., comp. *Columbus Geo., From Its Selection as a 'Trading Town' in 1827 to its Partial Destruction by Wilson's Raid in 1865.* Parts I and II. Columbus: Thomas Gilbert Pub., 1874. Reprint. N.p.: Georgia Genealogical Reprints, 1972.

Mealing, Mollie. *Century Old Houses of Columbus, Georgia and Vicinity.* Columbus: Columbus Office Supply Co., 1971.

Meyer, Henry Balthasar, ed. *History of Transportation in the United States before 1860.* Forge Village, Mass.: Murray Printing Co., 1948.

Miller, T. S., Sr. *The American Cotton System Historically Treated Showing Operations of the Cotton Exchanges.* Austin: Austin Printing Co., 1909.

Moore, Albert Burton. *History of Alabama.* University, Ala.: Alabama Book Store, 1934.

Morison, Samuel Eliot. *The Maritime History of Massachusetts, 1783–1860.* Boston: Houghton Mifflin Co., 1941.

Myers, Margaret G. *A Financial History of the United States.* New York: Columbia University Press, 1970.

———. *Origins and Development.* Vol. 1 of *The New York Money Market.* New York: Columbia University Press, 1931.

North, Douglass C. *The Economic Growth of the United States, 1790–1860.* Englewood Cliffs, N.J.: Prentice-Hall, 1961.

Otto, Rhea Cumming. *1850 Census of Georgia: Muscogee County.* N.p., 1977.

Parker, William P., ed. *The Structure of the Cotton Economy of the Antebellum South.* Baltimore: Waverly Press, 1970.

Perkins, Edwin J. *Financing Anglo-American Trade, The House of Brown,*

1800–1880. Cambridge, Mass., and London: Harvard University Press, 1975.
Perry, Joel W., comp. *Some Pioneer History of Early County, 1818–1871.* N.p.: N.d.
Phillips, Ulrich Bonnell. *A History of Transportation in the Eastern Cotton Belt to 1860.* New York: Columbia University Press, 1908. Reprint. New York: Octagon Books.
Porter, Glenn, ed. *Encyclopedia of American Economic History: Studies of the Principal Movements and Ideas.* Vol. 1. New York: Scribner's, 1980.
Porter, Louise M. *The Chronological History of the Lives of St. Joseph.* Chattanooga: Great American Publishing Co., 1975.
Price, Jacob. *Capital and Credit in British Overseas Trade, 1700–1776.* Cambridge: Harvard University Press, 1980.
*Problems of the Cotton Economy: Proceedings of the Southern Social Science Research Conference, New Orleans, March 8–9, 1935.* Dallas: Arnold Foundation, 1936.
Ratner, Sidney, James H. Soltow, and Richard Sylla. *The Evolution of the American Economy: Growth, Welfare, and Decision Making.* New York: Basic Books, 1979.
Redlich, Fritz. *The Molding of American Banking: Men and Ideas.* New York: Hafner Publishing Co., 1951.
Rogers, William Warren. *Outposts on the Gulf: Saint George Island and Apalachicola from Early Exploration to World War II.* Pensacola: University of West Florida Press, 1986.
Russel, Robert Royal. *Economic Aspects of Southern Sectionalism, 1840–1861.* Urbana: University of Illinois, 1924.
Schweikart, Larry. *Banking in the American South from the Age of Jackson to Reconstruction.* Baton Rouge: Louisiana State University Press, 1987.
Scott, Mrs. Marvin. *History of Henry County, Alabama.* Pensacola: Frank R. Parkhurst and Son, 1961.
Shofner, Jerrell H. *Daniel Ladd: Merchant Prince of Frontier Florida.* Gainesville: University Presses of Florida, 1978.
———. *Jackson County, Florida—A History.* Marianna, Fla.: Jackson County Heritage Association, 1985.
———. *Nor Is It Over Yet: Florida in the Era of Reconstruction.* Gainesville: University Presses of Florida, 1974.
Smart, Eugenia Persons. *History of Eufaula, Alabama.* Birmingham: Roberts and Sons, 1933.
Smith, Julia Floyd. *Slavery and Plantation Growth in Antebellum Florida, 1821–1860.* Gainesville: University of Florida Press, 1973.

Smith, Walter B., and Arthur H. Cole. *Fluctuations in American Business, 1790–1860*. Cambridge: Harvard University Press, 1935.

Standard, Diffy William. *Columbus, Georgia in the Confederacy.* New York: William-Frederick Press, 1954.

Stanley, J. Randall. *History of Jackson County.* N.p.: Jackson County Historical Society, 1950.

Stormont, John W. *The Economics of Secession and Coercion, 1861.* Victoria, Tex.: Victoria Advocate Publishing Co., 1957.

Summersell, Charles Grayson. *Mobile: History of a Seaport Town.* Mobile: University of Alabama Press, 1949.

Sumner, William Graham. *A History of American Currency.* New York: Holt and Co., 1874. Reprint. New York: William-Frederick Press, 1954.

———. *A History of Banking in the United States.* Vol. 1 of *A History of Banking in all the Leading Nations.* New York: Journal of Commerce and Commercial Bulletin, 1896.

Taylor, George Rogers. *The Transportation Revolution, 1815–1860.* Vol. 4 of *The Economic History of the United States.* New York: Harper and Row, 1951.

Telfair, Nancy [Louise Gunby Jones DuBose]. *A History of Columbus, Georgia, 1828–1928.* Columbus: Historical Publishing Co., 1929.

Temin, Peter. *The Jacksonian Economy.* New York: W. W. Norton, 1969.

Thompson, Mattie Thomas. *History of Barbour County, Alabama.* Eufaula: N.p., 1939.

Trescott, Paul B. *Financing American Enterprise: The Story of Commercial Banking.* New York: Harper and Row, 1963.

Turner, J. A. *The Cotton Planter's Manual: Being a compilation of Facts from the Best Authorities on the Culture of Cotton.* New York: C. M. Saxton and Co., 1857. Reprint. New York: Negro Universities Press, 1969.

Van Deusen, John G. *The Ante-Bellum Southern Commercial Convention.* Durham: Duke University Press, 1926.

Walker, Anne Kendrick. *Backtracking in Barbour County.* Richmond, Va.: Dietz Press, 1941.

———. *Russell County in Retrospect.* Richmond, Va.: Dietz Press, 1950.

Watkins, James L. *King Cotton: A Historical and Statistical Review, 1790–1908.* N.p.: James L. Watkins and Sons, 1908. Reprint. New York: Negro Universities Press, 1969.

White, George. *Historical Collections of Georgia.* New York: Pudney and Russell, 1854.

White, Horace. *Money and Banking.* 6th ed. Boston: Ginn and Co., 1936.

Whitehead, Margaret Laney, and Barbara Bogart. *City of Progress: A History of Columbus, Georgia, 1828–1928.* Columbus: Columbus Office Supply Press, 1979.

Williamson, Harold F., ed. *The Growth of the American Economy: An Introduction to the Economic History of the United States.* New York: Prentice-Hall, 1944.

Woodman, Harold D. *King Cotton and His Retainers: Financing and Marketing the Cotton Crop of the South, 1800–1925.* Lexington: University of Kentucky Press, 1968.

———. "Economy from 1815 to 1865." In Vol, 1 of *Encyclopedia of American Economic History: Studies of the Principal Movements and Ideas.* Edited by Glenn Porter. New York: Scribner's, 1980.

Worsley, Etta Blanchard. *Columbus on the Chattahoochee.* Columbus: Columbus Office Supply Co., 1951.

Wright, Buster W., comp. *Abstracts of Will Book "A," Muscogee County, Georgia, 1838–1862.* Columbus: Privately published, N.d.

Wright, Chester W. *Economic History of the United States.* New York: McGraw-Hill, 1941.

Wright, Gavin. *The Political Economy of the Cotton South: Households, Markets, and Wealth in the Nineteenth Century.* New York: W. W. Norton, 1978.

Young, Mary E. *Redskins, Ruffleshirts, and Rednecks.* Norman: University of Oklahoma Press, 1961.

## Articles

Albion, Robert G. "Early Nineteenth-Century Shipowning. A Chapter in Business Enterprise." *Journal of Economic History* 1, no. 1 (May 1941): 1–11.

Amos, Harriet E. "'Birds of Passage' in a Cotton Port: Northerners and Foreigners among the Urban Leaders of Mobile, 1820–1860." In *Class, Conflict, and Consensus: Antebellum Southern Community Studies,* edited by Orville Vernon Burton and Robert C. McMath, Jr. Westport, Conn.: Greenwood Press, 1982.

Atack, Jeremy, Fred Bateman, and Thomas Weiss. "Risk, the Rate of Return and the Pattern of Investment in Nineteenth Century American Manufacture." *Southern Economic Journal* 49, no. 1 (July 1982): 150–63.

Atherton, Lewis E. "The Problem of Credit Rating in the Ante-Bellum South." *Journal of Southern History* 12 (February–November 1946): 534–56.

Bickel, Karl A. "Robert E. Lee in Florida." *Florida Historical Quarterly* 27 (July 1948–April 1949): 59–66.

Callander, Guy S. "The Early Transportation and Banking Enterprises of the States in Relation to the Growth of the Corporation." *Quarterly Journal of Economics* 17 (1903): 111–62.

Chenault, William W., and Robert C. Reinders. "The Northern-born Community of New Orleans in the 1850s." *Journal of American History* 51, no. 2 (September 1964): 232–47.

Clark, T. D. "The Montgomery and West Point Railroad Company." *Georgia Historical Quarterly* 17, no. 1 (March 1933), 293–99.

*Columbus Magazine,* Vol. 4, no. 1 (September 30, 1943). This entire edition is on Chattahoochee steamboats.

Dodd, Dorothy. "The Manufacture of Cotton in Florida Before and During the Civil War." *Florida Historical Quarterly* 13, no. 1 (July 1934): 20–29.

Flanders, Ralph B. "Farish Carter, A Forgotten Man of the Old South." *Georgia Historical Quarterly* 15, no. 1 (March 1931): 142–72.

Ford, Lacy K. "Rednecks and Merchants: Economic Tension in the South Carolina Upcountry, 1865–1900." *Journal of American History* 71 (September 1984): 294–318.

Gallman, Robert E. "Self-Sufficiency in the Cotton Economy of the Antebellum South." In *The Structure of the Cotton Economy of the Antebellum South,* edited by William N. Parker. Baltimore: Waverly Press, 1970.

Goff, John H. "The Steamboat Period in Georgia." *Georgia Historical Quarterly* 12, no. 1 (March 1928): 236–54.

Govan, Thomas P. "Banking and the Credit System in Georgia, 1810–1860." *Journal of Southern History* 4 (May 1938): 164–84.

———. "Was Plantation Slavery Profitable." *Journal of Southern History* 8 (1942): 513–35.

Greenberg, Dolores. "Yankee Financiers and the Establishment of Trans-Atlantic Partnerships: A Re-examination." *Business History* 16 (1974): 17–35.

Haskins, Ralph W. "Planter and Cotton Factor in the Old South: Some Areas of Friction." *Agricultural History* 29 (January 1955): 1–14.

Hidy, Ralph W. "The Organization and Functions of Anglo-American Merchant Bankers, 1815–1860." *The Tasks of Economic History* (December 1941): 53–66. Supplement to *Journal of Economic History* 1 (May 1941).

Jordan, Weymouth T. "Cotton Planters' Conventions in the Old South." *Journal of Southern History* 19 (1953): 321–45.

Killick, John R. "The Cotton Operations of Alexander Brown and Sons in the Deep South, 1820–1860." *Journal of Southern History* 43, no. 2 (May 1977): 169–94.

———. "Bolton Odgen & Co.: A Case Study in Anglo-American Trade, 1790–1850." *Business History Review* 48 (Winter 1974): 501–19.

———. "Risk Specialization and Profit in the Mercantile Sector of the Nineteenth Century Cotton Trade: Alexander Brown and Sons, 1820–1880." *Business History* 16 (1974): 1–15.

Knetsch, Joe. "The Canal Era in West Florida: 1821–1845." *Gulf Coast Historical Review* 7, no. 1 (Fall 1991): 39–51.

———. "Canal Fever in North Florida." *Apalachee* 10 (1991): 40–53.

Kravis, Irving B. "The Role of Exports in 19th Century United States Growth." *Economic Development and Cultural Change* 20 (April 1972): 387–405.

Lindstrom, Diane. "Southern Dependence Upon Interregional Grain Supplies: A Review of the Trade Flows, 1840–1860." In *The Structure of the Cotton Economy of the Antebellum South*, edited by William N. Parker. Baltimore: Waverly Press, 1970.

Madison, James H. "The Evolution of Commercial Credit Reporting Agencies in Nineteenth-Century America." *Business History Review* 43 (Summer 1974): 164–86.

Marckhoff, Fred R. "The Development of Currency and Banking in Florida." *Coin Collector's Journal* (September–October 1947): 118–23.

Owens, Harry P. "Sail and Steam Vessels Serving the Apalachicola-Chattahoochee Valley." *Alabama Review* 21 (July 1968): 195–210.

Owsley, Frank L., and Harriet C. Owsley. "The Economic Bases of Society in the Late Ante-Bellum South." *Journal of Southern History* 6 (February–November 1940): 24–45.

Perkins, Edwin J. "Managing a Dollar-Sterling Exchange Account: Brown, Shipley and Co. in the 1850's." *Business History* 16 (1974): 48–64.

Schmidt, Lewis Bernard. "Internal Commerce and the Development of a National Economy Before 1860." *Journal of Political Economy* 47 (December 1939): 798–822.

Schuh, Niles, ed. "Apalachicola in 1838–1840: Letters from a Young Cotton Warehouse Clerk." *Florida Historical Quarterly* 68, no. 3 (January 1990): 312–23.

Schweikart, Larry. "Southern Banks and Economic Growth in the Antebellum Period: A Reassessment." *Journal of Southern History* 53, no. 1 (1987): 19–36.

Smith, Elizabeth F. "Apalachicola Steamboating During the Civil War." *Magnolia Monthly* (May 1973): unnumbered.

Smith, Joel P. "The Tavern: Older than Eufaula." *Lake Eufaula Guide* (June 1967).

Stone, Alfred H. "The Cotton Factorage System of the Southern States." *American Historical Review* 20, no. 1 (April 1915): 557–65.

Sylla, Richard. "American Banking and Growth in the Nineteenth Century: A Partial View of the Terrain." *Explorations in Economic History* 9, no. 2 (Winter 1971/72): 197–227.

Wender, Herbert. "The Southern Commercial Convention at Savannah, 1856." *Georgia Historical Quarterly* 15, no. 1 (March 1931): 142–72.

Whitman, Alice. "Transportation in Territorial Florida." *Florida Historical Quarterly* 17, no. 1 (July 1980): 25–53.

Woodman, Harold D. "Itinerant Cotton Merchants of the Antebellum South." *Agricultural History* 40, no. 2 (April 1966): 79–90.

## Unpublished Material

Chapel, George L. "Visitor's Center Raney House Museum Tour." Typescript at Apalachicola Chamber of Commerce.

Flewellen, Robert H. "The Tavern at Eufaula, Alabama (A Documentary)." Typescript. In "Alabama-Eufaula-Tavern" Folder. Carnegie Library, Eufaula, Alabama.

Hinton, E. H. "A Historical Sketch of the Evolution of Trade and Transportation at Columbus, Ga." Speech delivered at Belleair, Florida, 1912. Emory University Library.

Lovett, Rose Gibbons. "The Trilogy of Tri-Rivers: Apalachicola, Chattahoochee, and Flint." Typescript. In Lovett Family Papers. Florida State Archives. R. A. Gray Building. Tallahassee.

Lupold, John. "Some Preliminary Observations on the Textile and Water Powered Industries of Antebellum Columbus, Georgia." Paper submitted to National Endowment for the Humanities Seminar, University of North Carolina, Summer 1980.

McDonald, Cecil W. "The Economic History of Columbus, Georgia to the Civil War." Master's thesis. Auburn University, 1940.

Owens, Harry P. "Apalachicola Before 1861." Ph.D. diss., Florida State University, 1966.

————. "A History of Eufaula, Alabama, 1832–1882." Master's thesis, Auburn University, 1963.

Peddy, Thomas Joseph, comp. "Chattahoochee River Steamboats from Columbus, Georgia Newspapers." 10 vols. Handbound typescript, 1980. W. C. Bradley Memorial Library. Columbus, Georgia.

————, comp. "Reminiscences of Columbus by John E. Lamar." Handbound typescript, 1984. W. C. Bradley Memorial Library, Columbus, Georgia.

Thomas, David Yancey. "A History of Banking in Florida." Typed manuscript. Special Collections, Robert Manning Strozier Library, Florida State University, Tallahassee.

# Index

Flewellen, E. R., 21. *See also* Flewellen
  and Butt
Flewellen and Butt, 20
Flint River, 11, 13, 18, 19, 108, 109,
  117, 124, 133, 135; improvement of,
  126
Florida: banking regulations, 81
Florida Keys, 34, 36
Fort Gaines, Ga., 19, 27, 65; banks, 87;
  railroad projects, 126
*Franklin*, 118
Franklin, Ala., 19, 27
Fugitive Slave Law, 59

Galveston, Tex., 33, 115
*General Clinch*, 41, 48
General storekeepers, 6, 26–27
Georgia: banking regulations, 83–84
Goldstein and Co., 101
Gordon, A. C., and Co., 27
Greenwood and Grimes, 58
Gulf of Mexico, 5, 11, 12, 13, 32, 33,
  34, 36, 53, 117, 126, 127, 133
Gulf Stream, 34

Hall, H. T., 57
Hall and Deblois, 25
Harper and Holmes, 98
Havana, Cuba, 33, 38
Havre, France, 17, 33
Hawkins, George, 99
Hayward, Augustus, 108. *See also*
  Smith and Hayward
Heath, Milton Sydney, 123
*Henry*, 51
Henry County, Ala., 27, 73
Hill and Dawson, 108
Howard, John H., 105
Howard and Rutherford, 167 (n. 36)
Howell, John D., 57
Hurlbut, Elisha, 49
Hurlbut Packet Line, 49, 50

Insuring cotton, 29
Iola, Fla., 12
Irwinton Bridge Bank, 87

Jackson, Andrew, 71
Jamaica, 34
Jenkins, Capt. Edward B., 47

Kain, P. C., 107
Kain, William A., 94, 99, 107
*Kepler*, 36, 52
Key West, Fla., 33, 34, 36, 49, 52
Kimbrough, William H., 107, 109
Knowles, Capt. W. L., 34, 36

*Lamplighter*, 51
Lighthouses: on Dog Island, 33, 36; on
  Great Isaac Island, 36; on Key West,
  36; on St. George Island, 33; on Sand
  Cay, 36; on Sombrero Key, 36; on
  Tortugas, 36
*Lion*, 48
Liverpool, England, 14, 25, 33, 37, 38,
  39, 43, 49, 51, 93; commission mer-
  chants, 96; cotton market, 93
London, England, 90; money market,
  90
Lowell, Francis Cabot, 42
Lowell, Mass., 25
Lowell Warehouse, 25
Lumpkin, Ga., 119

Maclay, John C., 160 (n. 73)
Macon, Ga., 120, 122, 123, 124, 126,
  127, 133
Mallet, Capt. Edmond B., 47
Manchester, England, 14
Marianna, Fla., 18, 30, 119; economic
  conditions in, 73; private bankers
  in, 86
Marine and Fire Insurance Co., 160
  (n. 73)